A Nation
Gone Under

A Nation Gone Under

Robert C. Purvis IV

WESTBOW
PRESS*
A DIVISION OF THOMAS NELSON
& ZONDERVAN

WestBow Press books may be ordered through booksellers or by contacting:

WestBow Press
A Division of Thomas Nelson & Zondervan
1663 Liberty Drive
Bloomington, IN 47403
www.westbowpress.com
1 (866) 928-1240

ISBN: 978-1-5127-8435-0 (sc)
ISBN: 978-1-5127-8437-4 (hc)
ISBN: 978-1-5127-8436-7 (e)

Library of Congress Control Number: 2017906015

Print information available on the last page.

WestBow Press rev. date: 5/16/2017

Contents

Introduction..vii

CHAPTER 1   From Bibles to Birth Control: How
Christians Allowed the Moral Decline of
American Society... 1

CHAPTER 2   The Destruction of the Traditional Nuclear
Family..9

CHAPTER 3   The Takeover of Public Education 19

CHAPTER 4   The Takeover of Entertainment and
Mainstream Media 31

CHAPTER 5   The Attack on the First Amendment............. 37

CHAPTER 6   From Marxist Beginnings............................... 43

CHAPTER 7   The Fundamental Transformation of
America 51

CHAPTER 8   The Failure of the Opposition......................... 67

CHAPTER 9   Future Threats to Religious Freedom in
America 71

Conclusion 89

Introduction

The United States of America was birthed into existence based on founding principles rooted in the greatest devotion to liberty the world has ever seen. The most fundamental idea was that we possess natural inalienable rights simply by virtue of being human. The idea of inalienable rights asserted that government can neither grant such rights nor take them away. The US Constitution and the rights granted therein gave way to the greatest example of a free nation that history has to offer. It was a nation of people who championed principles such as hard work and personal responsibility, a country where individuals had the freedom to accomplish as much as their abilities would allow. But just as history has shown, freedom always becomes the target of tyrants. Over time, the seeds of neo-Marxism took root in America.

The first major deluge of socialist policies to befall America was brought by President Woodrow Wilson. Although the Progressive movement first arose in the late nineteenth century, it advanced significantly as a result of policies created by the Wilson administration. During his first year in office, the

Sixteenth Amendment (federal income tax) was ratified, and the Federal Reserve Act, which created and established the Federal Reserve System, was signed into law. Wilson was arguably the first American president to fully embrace a Marxist ideology. (World Net Daily, 2013) He did not respect American ideas nor the constitutional limited government, upon which such ideas are based.

He once wrote, "The trouble with the theory [of limited and divided government] is that government is not a machine, but a living thing. This is where the living and breathing constitution comes from. It is modified by its environment, necessitated by its tasks, shaped to its functions by the sheer pressure of life."

Socialism was drastically expanded by the New Deal, a series of domestic programs enacted between 1933 and 1938, during the first term of President Franklin D. Roosevelt. Programs created under the New Deal included the Social Security system, the US Housing Authority, and the Fair Labor Standards Act of 1938. The New Deal dramatically expanded the welfare state and created the first notions of an entitlement mentality within the American psyche. During his 1976 campaign for president, Ronald Reagan commented to the *New York Times* that "fascism was really the basis for the New Deal." Reagan later defended the comment, saying, "Anyone who wants to look at the writings of the Brain Trust of the New Deal will find that President Roosevelt's advisers admired the fascist system.... They thought that private ownership with government management and control à la the Italian system was the way to go, and that has been evident in all their writings." This was,

Reagan added, "long before fascism became a dirty word in the lexicon of the liberals."

Similarly to the New Deal, socialism was again promoted by the creation of the Great Society, a set of domestic programs launched by President Lyndon B. Johnson in 1964. The stated goal of the Great Society was to eliminate poverty and racial injustice. Regarding its stated purpose to fight poverty, the Great Society was arguably a failure. Not only did it further expand the welfare state, it had devastating effects on societal cornerstones such as work and marriage. Since the 1960s the employment rate among working-age men has declined significantly. In 2008 12 percent of American men ages thirty to forty-nine was absent from the labor force, compared to only 3 percent in 1968. Other negative trends include the erosion of marriage and the subsequent increase in the number of children born outside of marriage. Today over 40 percent of children are born to single mothers compared to under 10 percent in the 1960s. (Daily Signal, 2014)

The socialist policies of Democratic administrations during the twentieth century brought about major changes to the constitutionally limited form of government created by America's founders. Perhaps even more significant is the role such policies played in setting the stage for the types of communist policies that would come about in the future. After the fall of the Soviet Union in 1991, most of America erroneously believed communism was dead and no longer a threat. Communism became an afterthought in the minds of most Americans; they went about their lives enjoying a robust economy, which began during the latter part of the Reagan administration and carried on throughout the 1990s. However, the communist movement in America never died, and its members never conceded defeat. Instead, they simply retreated into the shadows, where they reassessed their approach to take over America. They abandoned the old idea of taking over America by means of an armed revolution and pivoted to a new idea of bringing America down from within. The new strategy consisted of infiltrating the institutions of America and acquiring positions of influence and power in order to fracture the system from the inside. They planned to incrementally bring about changes to the American way of life so slowly that most Americans would not realize the changes until it was too late.

In 1992 former Idaho Representative Curtis Bowers attended a gathering of the Communist Party USA at the University of California, Berkley. According to Bowers, the purpose of the meeting was to discuss the party's revised agenda to take over America. "The plan they unfolded had nothing to do with guns, bombs or violence. They acknowledged their disappointment with what had happened in the Soviet Union but felt they could still "take America down." This time, instead of using force from the outside, they would use public policy from the inside," wrote Bowers. "They had a three part agenda. They would use their manpower, influence and funds to back anything that would destroy our families, businesses and culture." (Idaho Press-Tribune, 2008)

During his Lyceum address in 1838, Abraham Lincoln warned of such danger from within: "At what point then is the approach of danger to be expected?" Lincoln asked. "I answer, if it ever reach us, it must spring up amongst us. It cannot come from abroad. If destruction be our lot, we must ourselves be its author and finisher. As a nation of freemen, we must live through all time, or die by suicide."

The following is an analysis of how successful the communist movement has been regarding its ultimate goal to take over America. As an accompanying guide, I have referenced the list of forty-five declared communist goals for the takeover of America, which first appeared in *The Naked Communist* written by W. Cleon Skousenwas in 1958 and was later introduced into Congressional Record by Congressman Albert S. Herlong Jr. in 1963.

Chapter 1

From Bibles to Birth Control: How Christians Allowed the Moral Decline of American Society

There was a time in America when Gideons were permitted to visit schools and pass out Bibles to students. In addition to distributing Bibles in classrooms, they were also permitted to briefly speak to each class. This would be inconceivable in today's society. Can you imagine the uproar that would follow if a school allowed Christian figures to pass out Bibles and then to take up time that is allotted for public education to speak about religion? The lawsuits would be endless. The liberal talking heads would immediately rant about religious indoctrination and a violation of the separation of church and state.

However, for two decades, Christians have been silent about the Progressive indoctrination that has swept our schools. Where were the lawsuits by Christians at the first sign of the Progressive assault on public education? Where were the Christians when the Gideons were denied entry into schools? They remained silent simply because liberals cloaked their attacks in a distortion of the Constitution. Instead of crying foul and pushing back against those who sought to twist our laws and use them against us, Christians chose to look the other way.

Now, two decades later, we are shocked to realize what has transpired. In 2007, *Fox News* reported that a school board in Portland, Maine, approved a proposal to begin issuing birth control to its middle school students. According to the report, "There are no national figures on how many middle schools, where most students range in age from eleven to thirteen, provide such services." This is, of course, in addition to middle schools also providing instruction on how to properly use condoms.

To accurately diagnose the current passive state of Christianity in America, one must first examine the process that led us to this point. There are many reasons why Christianity has fallen so far in such a short period of time, but perhaps none more significant than the lack of historical teaching among modern Christians. I believe the Bible to be a literal account of historical events; however, Christians should also be knowledgeable of the vast history that has taken place since biblical times. The postbiblical history of Christianity is largely ignored by most Christians today. This period of history is significant in that it helps us to understand many of the modern religious conundrums which Christians are facing today. For example, consider the rise in Islamic terrorism that has occurred in recent years. In order for Christians to properly grasp this issue, they must first be educated about the Crusades. Most Muslims view current global events as a continuation of the conflicts that occurred during the Crusades; therefore, to understand Islamic terrorism, one must first be able to view it in the context of that time period.

Beginning during the childhood years, the vast majority of Muslims are educated about the Crusades. In fact, literature about the Crusades is included in the curriculum of most Arab schools. In 2008, the *Washington Post* reported that Saudi textbooks contained inflammatory rhetoric that instructed Muslim students to hate Jews and Christians. Passages found in the text included "Jews and Christians are enemies" of Muslims, the Crusades never ended, and that Jews conspire to "gain sole control over the world." (*Washington Post*, 2008) The *Washington Post* article, which was based on a report by the Hudson Institute's Center for Religious Freedom, is just one of many to surface in recent years that shed light on the curriculum found in Islamic schools.

Even more disturbing to Americans should be the fact that such schools exist within the United States. A 2007 *Fox News* report stated that a congressionally mandated panel recommended the Bush administration close a Virginia-based Islamic school unless school officials complied with demands to turn over textbooks suspected of including lessons on "jihad and intolerance toward other religions." The report also cited a separate study conducted in 2006 by the Center for Religious Freedom which found that a ninth grade Saudi textbook "teaches teenagers in apocalyptic terms that violence towards Jews, Christians, and other unbelievers is sanctioned by God." (*Fox News*, 2006) Thus, not only are Muslims familiarized with the Crusades as children, they are also instructed to continue behavior that was common for that time period. When compared with the amount of attention given by Christians to the same historical time period, a clear distinction can be made.

A survey on religious knowledge conducted by the Pew Research Center found that while the United States is one of the most religious nations in the world, Americans are "uninformed about the tenets, practices, history, and leading figures of major faith traditions—including their own." Protestant Christians, who make up the nation's largest religion, averaged only 6.5 correct answers out of 12 questions regarding Christianity. According to the survey, "About half of Protestants (53%) cannot correctly identify Martin Luther as the person whose writings and actions inspired the Protestant Reformation, which made their religion a separate branch of Christianity." (Pew Research, 2010) Based on this statistical information, a valid argument can be made that modern American Christians are significantly ignorant of general historical facts regarding Christianity.

Another way in which Christians allowed moral decline to occur in American society is by complacency. In many countries, Christianity is suppressed and Christians are forced to worship in secrecy. Christians in such countries risk their lives simply to congregate and worship with one another. About two hundred million Christians are reportedly persecuted worldwide. A 2006 report by WorldNetDaily.com compiled a list of fifty countries that most severely persecute Christians. Also included in the report were details of persecutions ranging from false imprisonment to murder.

A culture in which such human rights violations exist is incomprehensible to most Christians born in the United States. From its creation, America has been an anomaly among global civilizations, offering as one of its founding principles the freedom of religion. However, centuries of such religious freedom has created a society of Christians who are oblivious to threats that seek to restrict, if not destroy, those freedoms. There is no better example of this than the American Civil Liberties Union (ACLU). In her 2006 article "ACLU's 'Search and Destroy' Agenda," Marsha West refers to the ACLU as the "devourer of religion" and equates it to a military search-and-destroy mission. She further stated, "The vast majority of Americans view the ACLU's hit-squad as God-haters that desire to destroy all vestiges of religion in the public square, and all Judeo-Christian values and beliefs."

Perhaps the most significant reason for the absence of Christians in the face of moral societal decline can be attributed to the rise of "pop Christianity." This watered-down version of Christianity has created a culture in America that is focused only on ideas that make individuals feel good about themselves. This pseudo-religion bears only a vague resemblance to the New Testament of the Bible. A religion that was founded by a man from humble beginnings who lived a life of meekness has become characterized by extravagant churches, where members attend services conducted in lavish settings. Equipped with features ranging from orchestras to big-screen TVs, today's church services more closely resemble Broadway presentations than opportunities for spiritual growth and worship. Despite fixations on extravagant buildings and flamboyant church services, the most damaging aspect of pop Christianity could be the ideas that it perpetuates.

With the rise of pop Christianity came the conception of mega churches, large churches in which pastors preside over enormous congregations. Possibly the most famous example is Joel Osteen, the pastor of Lakewood Church in Houston, which has the largest congregation in the United States. In addition to being a pastor, Osteen has written several self-help books, with the major emphasis on positive thinking. However, despite pastoring the largest church in the country and writing his share of best-selling books, Osteen never graduated from a seminary. So how does someone with no biblical training remain pastor of the largest church in the country? The answer is simple: by making people feel good and never forcing them to venture outside of their comfort zones. It is impossible to advance spiritually without challenging one's knowledge of faith. Therefore, Osteen is nothing more than a glorified motivational speaker.

Although Christians have no difficulty acknowledging the degree of moral decline in American society, the majority do not recognize their own contributing role through complacency and lackluster resistance toward negative societal reforms. By not confronting the Progressive agenda, which has sought to fundamentally change American society, Christians are partially responsible for the moral decline that has resulted from those changes. American Christians are rapidly approaching a point at which they will be forced to re-evaluate their perceptions of fundamental Christianity and decide what is more important: complacency gained by remaining within one's comfort zone, or the boldness to reject the shortcomings of mainstream Christianity. Until then, our society will remain one in which our schools not only forbid the acknowledgment of God but also encourage our children to live in direct contradiction to biblical principles.

Chapter 2

The Destruction of the
Traditional Nuclear Family

Since the creation of humanity, the family has been the fundamental unit of every civilization. In *The Mansions of Philosophy*, historian Will Durant wrote, "The family has been the ultimate foundation of every civilization known to history. It was the economic and productive unit of society, tilling the land together; it was the political unit of society, with parental authority as the supporting microcosm of the State. It was the cultural unit, transmitting letters and arts, rearing and teaching the young; and it was the moral unit, inculcating through cooperative work and discipline, those social dispositions which are the psychological basis and cement of civilized society."

This crucial role of the family within society was also understood by Karl Marx, who called for the abolition of the family structure. In *The Communist Manifesto*, Marx wrote, "The bourgeois family will vanish as a matter of course when its complement vanishes, and both will vanish with the vanishing of capital." He sought to bring about cultural change by destroying the history, customs, and traditions within society and viewed the family as standing in the way of such efforts. In fact, every proponent of the modern communist movement has agreed with Marxist theory that in order to accomplish desired cultural changes, the family must first be abolished.

The modern homosexual movement in America was founded by Henry Hay, a member of the Communist Party USA (CPUSA). Hay created an organization called the Mattachine Society, which was set up to infiltrate the culture of the United States to make homosexuality normal. Since the movement's inception, radical leaders have long sought to not only eradicate traditional marriage, but also change the cultural mind-set of our Judea-Christian society into one that is totally accepting of the homosexual lifestyle.

In the book *After the Ball: How America Will Conquer Its Fear and Hatred of Gays in the 1990s*, authors Marshall Kirk and Hunter Madsen outline a blueprint for gay activists that details how to apply brainwashing techniques that were developed by the totalitarian regime of Communist China. A further analysis of this program can be found in Robert Jay Lifton's 1989 book *Thought Reform and the Psychology of Totalism: A Study of Brainwashing in China*. According to Lifton, this system, which was created in Communist China and used by Kirk and Madsen, consists of three primary steps: desensitization, jamming, and conversion.

Desensitization is a process of getting the public accustomed to the idea of homosexuals being a normal part of their daily lives, through constant exposure of gays and lesbians on TV, in the movies, and in the media. Jamming is a process that involves shaming opponents into silence through accusations of bigotry and the fear of social stigmatization. Kirk and Madsen wrote, "All normal persons feel shame when they perceive that they are not thinking, feeling, or acting like one of the pack.... The trick is to get the bigot into the position of feeling a conflicting twinge of shame ... when his homohatred surfaces. Thus, propagandistic advertisement can depict homophobic and homohating bigots as crude loudmouths.... It can show them being criticized, hated, shunned. It can depict gays experiencing horrific suffering as the direct result of homohatred-suffering of which even most bigots would be ashamed to be the cause."

According to Kirk and Madsen, this tactic doesn't even require the use of facts: "Our effect is achieved without reference to facts, logic, or proof. Just as the bigot became such, without any say in the matter, through repeated infralogical emotional conditioning, his bigotry can be alloyed in exactly the same way, whether he is conscious of the attack or not. In short, jamming succeeds insofar as it inserts even a slight frisson of doubt and shame into the previously unalloyed, self-righteous pleasure. The approach can be quite useful and effective—if our message can get the massive exposure upon which all else depends."

The process of conversion is intended to change the heart of the public so that it becomes more receptive to the gay agenda. Kirk and Madsen wrote, "Conversion aims at just this ... conversion of the average American's emotions, mind, and will, through a planned psychological attack, in the form of propaganda fed to the nation via the media." (Renew America, 2004)

Communist Goal 26. Present Homosexuality, Degeneracy, and Promiscuity as "Normal, Natural, and Healthy"

Another effective tool used to by the communist movement to destroy the family has been the feminist movement. Betty Friedan is credited as being the founder of modern feminism. The purpose of the movement was to attack full-time homemakers and convince women they were victims of an oppressive, unjust patriarchy. While also at the time peddling her book *The Feminine Mystique*, Friedan portrayed herself as a frustrated housewife who simply wanted to help other women. However, in the 1990s, it was revealed that she had been a radical propagandist for the Communist Party. In 1943, Friedan dropped out of grad school at the University of California, Berkeley to become a journalist for leftist and union publications, which included the Federated Press and the *United Electrical Workers' News*. Therefore, when Friedan described the traditional American family as "a comfortable concentration camp," she did so as a result of her Marxist beliefs rather than her experience as a housewife. Friedan went on to cofound several communist organizations such as the National Organization for Women, the National Association for the Repeal of Abortion Laws, and National Women's Political Caucus, all of which were front organizations designed to destroy the institution of the family.

Following Friedan's anti-family mantra, the feminist movement began to grow and intensify its attack on traditional family values. Sheila Cronan, a respected leader of the feminist movement, said, "Since marriage constitutes slavery for women, it is clear that the women's movement must concentrate on attacking marriage." Beginning in the 1960s and 1970s, radical feminists launched an assault on national laws that for more than a century had protected the institution of marriage. Within a few years, they succeeded in overturning "fault divorce" laws in all fifty states in the nation and replaced them with "no-fault divorce." It was portrayed as an effort to provide women with the same economic, social, and political rights as men. However, as Lenora Weitzman wrote in her book *The Divorce Revolution*, abolishing "divorce laws reinforced those responsibilities, rewarding spouses who fulfilled their marital obligations and punishing those who did not." By abolishing "the concept of fault, it also eliminated the framework of guilt, innocence and … the law's condemnation of marital misconduct." The advent of "convenience" divorces weakened the institution of marriage and changed the cultural view of divorce. A 2008 Gallup poll found that cultural tolerance for divorce grew from 59 percent in 2001 to 70 percent in 2008.

Communist Goal 40. Discredit the Family as an Institution; Encourage Promiscuity and Easy Divorce

On August 14, 1935, President Franklin D. Roosevelt signed the Social Security Act into law, describing it as a "cornerstone" of the modern welfare state. Since then, both parties have passed legislation expanding government entitlements; however, the Progressive Left saw it as an opportunity to further their communist agenda. By creating a society of dependency, communists operating under the guise of "progressivism" began to use the welfare system to break down low-income families, which became dependent on government subsidies. Nowhere was this more prevalent than within the black community. Dr. Walter Williams, an economist at George Mason University, writes in his autobiography *Up from the Projects,* "The welfare state has done to black Americans what slavery couldn't do … and that is to destroy the black family." Reflecting on his childhood in the Richard Allen housing projects in Philadelphia, Dr. Williams writes, "My father deserted us when I was three and my sister was two. But we were the only kids who didn't have a mother and father in the house. These were poor black people and a few whites living in a housing project, and it was unusual not to have a mother and father in the house. Today, in the same projects, it would be rare to have a mother and father in the house." Even during the antebellum period, when many slaves where prohibited from marrying, most black children lived with both biological parents. From reconstruction until the 1940s, between 75 and 85 percent of black children lived in two-parent households. Today, the number of black children born to single women is more than 70 percent. (Wall Street Journal, 2011)

In a 2011 *Fox News* interview, Star Parker, author of *Uncle Sam's Plantation: How Big Government Enslaves America's Poor,* said that welfare dependency destroyed the black family. "After the war on poverty in the 1960s, we began to see the unraveling of the entire black community because the family collapsed," said Parker. She further stated that during the 1960s, the black family was healthy, with 78 percent of husbands living in the home, but it declined after the federal government began to reward couples for being unmarried and unemployed. "Over time marriage stopped occurring to where now 7 out of 10 black children are born outside of marriage, and what happens when you don't have that intact family is your values change. So your culture changes. So your community changes," said Parker.

A 2015 survey released by the Family Research Council's Marriage and Religion Research Institute showed that "just 17 percent of black teens live with their nuclear family, an all-time low and down from 38 percent in 1950." (Washington Examiner, 2015)

An increasing number of African Americans are realizing that what has been portrayed for decades by many on the Left as liberal compassion has been nothing more than a ploy to dismantle the black family, in an effort to destroy the culture, thereby creating a permanent voting bloc that was solely dependent on government. Of course, the issue of government dependency has not been restricted solely to the black community. While the black family has been a specific target, the idea of an entitlement society is one that has been promoted by the Left for decades, until today it permeates all of American society. Like any good Marxist, those on the Left know that the more a society depends on government, the less likely the people are to rise up against it. Today, one in five Americans—67 million—rely on some type of federal aid.

The expansion of the welfare state, combined with a decline in morality, has taken a devastating toll on the traditional nuclear family. According to 2015 data published by the US Census Bureau, there were more married couples with children in the United States in 1963 than there were in 2014. Fifty-two years

ROBERT C. PURVIS IV

ago, there were 24.3 million married couples in America who had at least one child under eighteen living in the household, according to bureau statistics. In 2014, despite a significantly larger national population, there were only 23.9 million. In 1957, there were 49.7 million households in the United States, according to Census statistics, and 22.1 million of them (44.6 percent) consisted of a mother and a father and one or more children. In 2014, there were 123.2 million households in the United States with only 23.9 million (19.4 percent) consisting of a mother and a father and one or more children. (Town Hall, 2015)

The communist Left has also made great strides in destroying the traditional family by promoting sexual promiscuity. Today's families are bombarded with propaganda designed to normalize promiscuity and entice adults, as well as adolescents, to engage in polyamory. A 2004 study published in *Pediatrics*, the American Academy of Pediatrics journal, linked teen pregnancy to watching TV shows containing sexual content. The research suggested teens who viewed television programs containing a lot of sexual content were twice as likely to become involved sexually at a younger age than teens who watched less. Lead researcher, psychologist Rebecca Collins, told Reuters News, "This is the strongest evidence yet that the sexual content of television programs encourages adolescents to initiate sexual intercourse and other sexual activities." If a show talks about sex, rather than revealing it explicitly, the outcome is just as pronounced. "Both affect adolescents' perceptions of what is normal sexual behavior and propels their own sexual behavior," Collins revealed. (Catholic Exchange, 2004) Polyamory is even being taught on college campuses, as progressivism has taken over our nation's universities.

As of 2016, universities across the country began actively encouraging students to be more "affirming" of nonmonogamous relationships and instructing them to view polyamorous relationships as an acceptable lifestyle choice. Portland State University, the University of Michigan, and Columbia University all held events promoting acceptance of polyamorous relationships. Vanderbilt University sponsored a workshop titled "Deconstructing Couplehood" that was advertised as "a crash course in polyamory." Students who participated in the workshop would "deconstruct the 'ideal' and privileged relationship and look towards the other myriad ways to love and form community." (Daily Caller, 2016)

Also, the University at Albany-SUNY sponsored a monthly polyamorous talk, where students were invited to come "talk about the practice, desire, or acceptance of having more than one intimate relationship at a time with the knowledge and consent of everyone involved." Similarly, the University of California at Berkeley held a three-part series on polyamory and nonmonogamy. (Daily Caller, 2016)

Just as Marx instructed, the modern communist movement has carried out a vigorous assault on the traditional nuclear family, and certainly the case can be made that it has had significant success. The homosexual movement, the feminist movement, and the welfare state have merely been tools used by the communist movement to abolish the institution of the family. The concept of marriage is demeaned by the communist Left as antiquated, while polyamory is encouraged as natural sexual behavior. What Karl Marx referred to as the "bourgeois family" was simply the biblical family. The communist movement seeks to destroy traditional marriage because the ability to engineer a utopian society is impeded by the values of our Judea-Christian civilization, which are taught through marriage. Perhaps the one thing that will prevent the communist Left from achieving its agenda is a healthy, strong nuclear family.

Chapter 3

The Takeover of Public Education

A primary target of any communist effort to bring down a country is always the children. John Dewy is regarded as having been the most influential man in the area of public education; he is often referred to as "the father of modern education." After traveling to Russia in 1928 to study the educational system designed by Karl Marx, he returned to the United States and began to implement the same style of education. Dewy was an atheist/socialist/ humanist who believed that public education should be used to socialize children to make them willing wards of the state.

The Marxist transformation of the educational system in the United States that began with Dewy in the early 1900s was drastically expanded in the 1960s, due to the Far Left gaining control of the teacher's unions as well as the universities. The National Education Association (NEA), which has completely embraced the radical socialist ideas of the 1960s, has set forth a curriculum that is intended to train children in such a way that they will ultimately become wards of the state. In his book *Toward Soviet America*, William Z. Foster stated, "Among the elementary measures the American Soviet government will adopt to further the cultural revolution are the following: the schools, colleges and universities will be coordinated and grouped under the National Department of Education and its state and local branches. The studies will be revolutionized, being cleansed of religious, patriotic and other features of the bourgeois ideology. The students will be taught on the basis of Marxian dialectical materialism, inter-nationalism and the general ethics of the new socialist society. Present obsolete methods of teaching will be superseded by a scientific pedagogy." The curriculum that is currently being taught in public schools throughout the United States would shock and disturb most parents. Some of the following material is included in the curriculum:

- earth worship (pantheism)
- evolution
- socialized medicine
- world government
- animal rights (animals seen as brothers and sisters)
- redistribution of American wealth to other nations
- contraception and reproductive health (legal abortion)
- debt forgiveness for third world nations
- adoption of the gay rights agenda
- the elimination of the right to bear arms
- setting aside massive amounts of private land where no human presence is allowed

Most Americans have no knowledge of secular humanism, despite the fact it has existed for almost a century. The humanism movement originated at the University of Chicago in the 1920s and was introduced to the public in the 1933 publication of the first *Humanist Manifesto*. In 1943, the American Humanist Association (AHA) was established in Illinois as a nonprofit organization; it has had a profound influence on American education ever since. *The Humanist Manifesto I*, which states the beliefs of the AHA, was signed by thirty-four authors and educators, including John Dewy. It was the declaration of an entirely secular religion, which at the time even employed the term "religion" to describe the movement. The philosophy of the AHA had a major influence on the National Education Association. An article titled "A Religion for a New Age," which appeared in the *Humanist*, the official publication of the AHA, stated, "The Bible is an incredibly dangerous book ... the battle for humankind's future must be waged and won in the public classroom by teachers who correctly perceive their role as the proselytizers of a new faith ... the classroom must and will become an arena of conflict between the old and the new- the rotting corpse of Christianity, together with all its adjacent evils and misery, and the new faith of humanism, resplendent with the promise of a world in which the never-realized Christian ideal of 'love thy neighbor' will finally be achieved."

In 2009, the NEA passed a resolution endorsing gay marriage and adoption in states where legal (in other words, supporting and promoting the homosexual agenda). The NEA also recommended that gay, lesbian, bisexual, and transgendered issues become required content for teacher qualification. In other words, teachers would be forced to undergo sensitivity training regarding homosexuality before becoming certified to teach. Another decision by the NEA was to replace the word "tolerance" toward homosexuality with the word "acceptance." In essence, the NEA has declared that tolerance of the homosexual lifestyle is not enough, but that it must be accepted and respected. Children as young as first grade are now being indoctrinated with books such as *Heather Has Two Mommies*, *Daddy's Roommate*, and *Gay Pride Parade*.

Another popular form of indoctrination currently being forced upon our children is the ideal of globalism. Many schools now promote earth worship to children under the guise of environmental awareness. An increased number of schools now teach some form of a "world pledge," which was preceded by a similar pledge that is taught to our children on Earth Day each April. It's important to understand that the very concept Earth Day itself is steeped in communist ideology. The very date itself, April 22, is the birthday of Vladimir Lenin, founder of the Soviet Union. The first Earth Day was held on April 22, 1970, which was also the hundredth anniversary of the birth of the communist Bolshevik leader. The event was organized by a college professor named Paul Ehrlich and Democratic Senator Gaylord Nelson of Wisconsin. Ehrlich had written a book titled *Population Bomb*, published in 1968, which warned of major societal upheavals due to overpopulation and advocated "brutal and heartless decisions" to limit population growth. (World Net Daily, 2012)

Ehrlich stated, "We must have population control at

home, hopefully through changes in our value system, but by compulsion if voluntary methods fail." Having been inspired by the book, Sen. Nelson met with Ehrlich, and the two came up with the idea of a "nationwide teach-in" with the purpose of utilizing the "environmental concerns of the general public and infuse the student anti-war energy into the environmental cause." In the book *Eco-Tyranny: How the Left's Green Agenda will Dismantle America*, author Brian Sussman states, "During Lenin's reign, Russia initiated the most audacious nature conservancy program in the twentieth century. Starting with a vision created by Marx 50 years prior, Lenin had successfully implemented version one of the green agenda. His accomplishments would eventually … [be] celebrated the world over each April." (World Net Daily, 2012)

The Global, Learning and Observations to Benefit the Environment (GLOBE) Program consists of organizations such as Green Cross International (which is headed by Mikhail Gorbachev, former leader of the Soviet Union), UNESCO (which is the source of most of the anti-American curriculum), and the International Baccalaureate. The GLOBE Program is funded and implemented through the federal Department of Education. It was created under Goals 2000, a grant program intended to promote higher standards for student learning, and was carried over in No Child Left Behind.

In a further effort to capture the minds of America's youth, the Department of Education announced in 2009 the beginning of a contest called Race to the Top, which was funded by $4.35 billion in stimulus funds. Within three years of the announcement, many parents, teachers, and governors came to a terrible realization, that these would be the likely outcomes of the "contest":

- regionalism, or the replacement of local governments by federally appointed bureaucrats
- a leveling of all schools to one, low national standard, and a redistribution of education funds among school districts
- an effective federal tracking of all students
- the loss of the option of avoiding the national curriculum and tests through private school and home school

However, the most dangerous component of Race to the Top was a yet-to-be-written standard for curriculum called Common Core. Absurdly enough, governors committed to the contest without first knowing what the Common Core standards would consist of. Smarter Balanced Assessment Consortium and Partnership for Assessment Readiness of College and Careers, each a coalition of states intended to create educational assessments, was given $360 million in federal funds to create national Common Core-aligned tests and curriculum models. On August 12, 2012, the Department of Education offered yet another competition for $400 million in Race to the Top funds for local districts to "personalize learning, close achievement gaps and take full advantage of twenty-first-century tools." The fed's announcement aligned with Common Core's emphasis on leveling of achievement and personalized learning. In the text selection of the *Publishers' Criteria for the Common Core State Standards,* guide B mandates that "all students (including those who are behind) have extensive opportunities to encounter grade-level complex text." (Accuracy in Media, 2012)

By 2013, opposition began to emerge as people learned more about Common Core. Soon, it caught the attention of conservative groups, who saw it as a major intrusion into public education by extreme left-wing entities. Proponents of the standards fought back by launching a media campaign to promote Common Core and cast it in a positive light. Millions were spent throughout various states to promote Common Core in an effort to sway public opinion.

Perhaps the single most destructive change to public school curriculum is the altering (or in some cases complete replacement) of the teaching of traditional American history. The absence of an adequate curriculum of our nation's history will have far reaching and extremely devastating effects on the future of American culture. As part of Common Core's K-12 literacy standards, US history was combined with English language arts (ELA). A 2014 study published by the Pioneer Institute (PI), a Boston-based research group, highlighted serious concerns regarding the merging of academic disciplines. A PI press release about the study stated, "By trying to include U.S. History in English language arts standards, Common Core will further damage history instruction." The study was also critical of the recently issued new Advanced Placement (AP) US history curriculum. "The College Board's new A.P. U.S. History curriculum further mirrors the ideological biases of Progressive education. It begins with a series of negative and divisive themes that are heavily focused on the balkanizing formation of gender, class, racial, and ethnic identity politics," read the PI press release. (Pioneer Institute, 2014)

In August 2014, the College Board, which oversees various AP exams (including the SAT), implemented new framework for the AP US history exam that forced schools to transform the way American history is taught.

The new framework, which dictated how teachers were to cover the required material, presented a negative view of American history. It made little mention of the founding fathers and only a vague reference to the Declaration of Independence. It highlighted racism and oppression while ignoring the founding principles which gave birth to the freest nation in the history of humanity. The redesigned framework also usurped the power of state governments by overriding any existing state history standards. Despite claims from College Board spokespeople insisting that the framework would allow the flexibility to teach state-mandated material, the College Board's own website confirmed that the new AP history exam would focus exclusively on content specified in the framework. (Breitbart, 2014) It is important to note that the president of the College Board, David Coleman, was also a chief architect of Common Core and the principal author of its ELA standards.

Communist Goal 29. Discredit the American Constitution by Calling It Inadequate, Old-Fashioned, Out of Step with Modern Needs, a Hindrance to Cooperation between Nations on a Worldwide Basis

Goal 30. Discredit the American Founding Fathers. Present Them as Selfish Aristocrats Who had No Concern for the "Common Man."

Goal 31. Belittle All Forms of American Culture and Discourage the Teaching of American History on the Ground that It Was Only a Minor Part of the Big Picture.

The education of a nation's youth has been a major target of every communist movement. Vladimir Lenin, founder of the Soviet Union, stated, "Give me four years to teach the children and the seed I have sown will never be uprooted." In Nazi Germany, Adolf Hitler created the Hitler Youth. The first step to improving education must be to take the federal government out of it. Article I, section 8 of the US Constitution, which grants the federal government all of the powers it has, does not give the federal government any power to control education. Since the US Department of Education was created in 1979, education has not improved but has arguably declined due to incessant tampering and restrictions by the federal government. Almost everything that William Z. Foster wanted included in the public school curriculum has been accepted by today's public schools. Government schools now consist of a Progressive form of education that focuses on social ideas rather than teaching actual facts of history, science, and mathematics. Social engineering is used to train children to think collectively. Common Core was intended to ultimately dictate curriculum that would indoctrinate our children with communist ideas, predisposing them to accept a totalitarian form of government.

Control of public education must be given back to state and local governments, as it was intended. Parents must become engaged and push back against any and all indoctrination that exists within our public schools. A workforce preparedness program should also be created in schools to give kids who are not serious about their education the choice to opt out of the traditional classroom and learn a trade. This would guarantee those who choose the aforementioned route a job once they complete high school because they would possess a particular skill. Students who do not want to be in the classroom are often a distraction to those who do. Giving students the option to opt out of the traditional classroom in order to learn a trade would benefit students who want to be there and receive a traditional education. We must stop the unrealistic expectation that every child should go to college (or even wants to). The fact is, not every child is college material and therefore should not be pressured into attending college simply to meet a liberal utopian idea that every child is the same. The Far Left seeks to use public education to create a society of people who are so dumbed down that they are unable to care for themselves or rise up against any incidence of government oppression. Once a certain percentage of the population falls into that category, our constitutionally limited form of government will no longer be sustainable.

Communist Goal 17. Get Control of the Schools. Use Them as Transmission Belts for Socialism and Current Communist Propaganda. Soften the Curriculum. Get Control of Teachers' Associations. Put the Party Line in Textbooks

Goal 28. Eliminate Prayer or Any Phase of Religious Expression in the Schools on the Ground that It Violates the Principle of Separation of Church and State

Goal 41. Emphasize the Need to Raise Children away from the negative influence of parents. Attribute Prejudices, Mental Blocks and Retarding of Children to Suppressive Influence of Parents

Chapter 4

The Takeover of Entertainment and Mainstream Media

In *Primetime Propaganda,* author Ben Shapiro makes the case that influential figures within the TV industry use their positions to promote a liberal agenda. Shapiro argues that popular TV shows including *Friends, Glee, The Golden Girls, Charlie's Angels, Desperate Housewives, The Mary Tyler Moore Show, Three's Company* and *Roseanne* contained propaganda to further a liberal political agenda. Shapiro bases his case on comments made by Hollywood executives, producers, and writers in thirty-nine taped interviews. *Friends* creator and writer Marta Kauffman said she "put together a staff of mostly liberal people," therefore making a liberal agenda inevitable on the show. Kauffman also said she created a role specifically to antagonize conservatives. When Candace Gingrich, half-sister of former Republican House Speaker Newt Gingrich, was cast as the minister at a lesbian wedding, "there was a bit of a [expletive deleted] you in it to the right wing," said Kauffman. (Daily Mail, 2011) Susan Harris, creator of *The Golden Girls,* said, "If we could inject some social reality, and make some points, that was terrific … [and] the best way to really approach threatening topics was through humor.… You could get away with more." She also referred to conservatives as "idiots" with "medieval minds." Marc Cherry, creator of *Desperate Housewives*, talked about using the show to push gay rights. "One of the things I'm proudest about is the addition of the gay neighbors on Wisteria Lane," he said. "To me that became its own political statement, which was see, 'You can have gay neighbors and they can be perfectly fine, and fit in with the rest of the folks, and it doesn't change anything.' And you kind of hope that you are preparing the way, planting little seeds in the minds of people."

Another example of propaganda was the effort to promote Obamacare within primetime television shows. In 2012, Covered California, the agency responsible for implementing Obamacare within the state, paid $900,000 to the global marketing powerhouse Ogilvy Public Relations Worldwide to promote the health care law within popular TV shows, including *Grey's Anatomy* and *Modern Family*. According to a report by the *New York Times*, Ogilvy planned to use prime-time television shows by weaving the health care law into their plots. "I'd like to see 10 of the major TV shows, or telenovelas, have people talking about 'that health insurance thing,'" said Peter V. Lee, the exchange's executive director. "There are good story lines here." (Townhall, 2014)

Still, perhaps the best example of left-wing bias may be that of the mainstream media's coverage of news events. Consider the mainstream media's tendency to automatically cast speculation toward the conservative movement each time an act of violence occurs that garners national attention. For example, on January 8, 2011, Congresswoman Gabriel Giffords was the victim of an assassination attempt while speaking to constituents near Tucson, Arizona. The mainstream media wasted no time attempting to blame conservatives for the attack. NBC's Lee Cowan suggested the Giffords shooting was motivated by Sarah Palin's website map featuring crosshairs on Giffords' district. "Not since Timothy McVeigh attacked the federal building in Oklahoma City has a crime sparked so much attention on anti-government rhetoric. That map Sarah Palin put up on Facebook last year, targeting Congresswoman Gifford's seat, made Giffords nervous, even then," said Cowan. In a story titled "Crosshairs Controversy: Palin Criticized for 'Targeting Giffords,'" NBC's Andrea Mitchell said, "The attack has reopened criticism of the way Palin targeted Gabby Giffords and 19 other Democrats in last year's campaign."

MSNBC's Chris Matthews attempted to link Sarah Palin and Michelle Bachman to the shooting, saying, "Sarah Palin using gun play language. What is she talking about crosshairs and reloading … and Bachmann out there with her kind of talk. I mean it seems like the way people talk now has, has gotten more ballistic.... Why are guns talked about so much, especially on the right? Why?"

When two Islamic terrorists attacked the Boston Marathon on April 15, 2013, the mainstream media once again rushed to speculate conservatives were behind the attack. CNN national security analyst Peter Bergen speculated that "right-wing extremists" could be behind the attack. MSNBC's Chris Matthews told viewers that "as a category, normally, domestic terrorists tend to be on the Far Right." *Esquire's* Charles P.

Piers wrote, "Obviously, nobody knows anything yet, but I would caution folks jumping to conclusions about foreign terrorism to remember that this is the official Patriots Day holiday in Massachusetts, celebrating the Battles at Lexington and Concord, and that the actual date (April 19) was of some significance to, among other people, Tim McVeigh, because he fancied himself a waterer of the tree of liberty and the like."

In November 2015, when a lone gunman killed three people at a Planned Parenthood clinic in Colorado Springs, the mainstream media rushed to characterize the gunman as a conservative white Christian Republican, before law enforcement had released the slightest details about the perpetrator. CNN commentator Sally Kohn on Twitter blamed the murders on the "rhetoric" of the "anti-abortion Right." Brett Gleason, a *Huffington Post* blogger, demanded that "selfrighteous white Christians [sic] please just admit that they have plenty of their own terrorists." Norm Goldman, a radio talk show host, tweeted, "Republicans have yet more blood on their hands." Heather Hogan, a senior editor for Autostraddle, a lesbian feminist website, tweeted, "If you can differentiate [between] Christians and the white dude who shot up Planned Parenthood, you can differentiate [between] Muslims and ISIS."

Also compare and contrast the media's coverage of the Tea Party with that of the short-lived Occupy Wall Street movement, which sprang up in 2011. Throughout the media, members of the Tea Party were denounced as right-wing extremists and in many cases even referred to as terrorists. In 2011 *Politico* ran an Op-Ed titled, *The Tea Party's Terrorist Tactics*, which featured an illustration of an individual with a dollar sign-shaped bomb strapped to their chest. TIME featured a piece written by Joe Klein in which he accused Republicans of being beholden to "Tea Party robots." In reference to their perceived unwillingness to compromise, Klein wrote that were he still alive, Osama bin Laden "could not have come up with a more clever strategy for strangling our nation." In an Op-Ed for *Politico* titled *The Tea Party Taliban*, Former Democratic Congressman, Martin Frost, argued that "like the Taliban" the Tea Party viewed "compromise as an unacceptable alternative." In an Op-Ed piece for the New York Times, Thomas Friedman described Tea Party Republicans as "Hezbollah." Peter Goodman at the Huffington Post wrote "They are acting like terrorists. Yes, terrorists."

The mainstream media failed to report the more than four hundred crimes committed by Occupiers during nationwide protests. Incidents that occurred at Occupy events included rapes, thefts, drug abuse, rampant property damage, gun violence, and even deaths. Also ignored by the media was the long list of anti-American groups that funded Occupy protests. Such groups included Communist Party USA, American Nazi Party, Socialist Party USA, Council on American Islamic Relations (CAIR), Party for Socialism and Liberation, Freedom Road Socialist Organization, and International Socialist Organization. World leaders who verbally expressed support for the movement included Hugo Chavez, Louis Farrakhan, Ayatollah Khamenei, and President Barack Hussein Obama.

Yet despite degenerate behavior by protesters and its affiliation with anti-American groups, the Occupy Wall Street movement was praised by the mainstream media. Instead, the media desperately sought to portray the Tea Party as the real threat. In 2010, the Media Research Center released a report titled *TV's Tea Party Travesty: How ABC, CBS and NBC Have Dismissed and Disparaged the Tea Party Movement,* which looked at coverage of the Tea Party during its first year of existence. Among its findings was that networks aired only sixty-one stories about the Tea Party over a twelve-month period. The report also found that 44 percent of stories "suggested the movement reflected a fringe or dangerous quality."

Communist Goal 20. Infiltrate the Press. Get Control of Book Review Assignments, Editorial Writing, Policymaking Positions

Goal 21. Gain Control of Key Positions in Radio, TV, and Motion Pictures

Anytime a government engages in propaganda, it should raise concerns, but particularly when it does so using taxpayer money.

Chapter 5

The Attack on the First Amendment

In order for communism to thrive, it must eradicate all forms of dissent, especially the freedom of speech. Our founding fathers listed free speech first within the Bill of Rights because they understood its importance in relation to all other freedoms. Unfortunately, free speech in America is becoming increasingly restricted under the guise of political correctness.

By working in collusion with the mainstream media, the communist Left controls the narrative by allowing the spread of news that supports their agenda. This type of governmental effort to deceive and control the people is reminiscent of George Orwell's novel *1984*. In the book, Orwell coined the term "newspeak" in reference to controlled language by a totalitarian government, which consisted of reinventing the meaning of ordinary words while attempting to rewrite the past. In reality, this is often referred to as wordsmithing. Under the Obama administration, similar Orwellian tactics were used to control public sentiment.

For example, illegal aliens became "undocumented

immigrants," semiautomatic rifles became "weapons of war," and conservatives became "right-wing extremists." Media pundits quickly labeled anyone who disagreed with their liberal positions as "racist," "sexist," "homophobic," "Islamophobic," "xenophobic," and so on, in an effort to shame those with opposing views into being silent. For example, the media constantly protected Obama by refusing to report the facts surrounding his administration, while labeling anyone who dared to criticize him as a "racist."

In 2010, MSNBC's Keith Olbermann accused critics of Obama's State of the Union address of being racists for using "code words" such as "cocky," "flippant," and "arrogant." "When there's a risk even in saying 'uppity' or 'forgetting his place,' the racist white guys revert to euphemisms and code words. And among the code words that they think they're getting away with are 'cocky,' 'flippant,' 'punk,' and especially 'arrogant,'" said Olbermann.

In 2013, another MSNBC host, Chris Matthews, accused Obama's critics of being motivated by "white supremacy." "And they can't stand the idea that a man who's not white is president. That is real. That sense of racial superiority and rule is in the hearts of some people in this country. Not all conservatives, not even all right-wingers, but it always comes through," said Matthews.

While appearing on *Fox News Sunday* in 2014, liberal commentator Juan Williams suggested those who were calling for Obama's impeachment were driven by racism. "The core constituency—the people who want him impeached—they're almost all white, and they're all older, and guess what? They're all in the Far Right Wing of the Republican Party," said Williams. (Daily Caller, 2014)

Also in 2014, Attorney General Eric Holder suggested that critics of the Obama administration were motivated by race. While speaking before Al Sharpton's National Action Network, Holder told the audience that he was proud of the significant strides and lasting reforms his department had achieved "even in the face of unprecedented, unwarranted, ugly, and divisive adversity." "You look at the way the Attorney General of the United States was treated yesterday by a House Committee. It had nothing to do with me. Forget about that. What Attorney General has ever had to deal with that kind of treatment? What president has ever had to deal with that kind of treatment?" said Holder. (Freebeacon, 2014) Later that year, Holder again played the race card in an interview with *ABC News* by claiming that he and Obama had long been the target of "racial animus." "There's a certain level of vehemence, it seems to me, that's directed at me [and] directed at the president," Holder told ABC. "You know, people talking about taking their country back.... There's a certain racial component to this for some people. I don't think this is the thing that is a main driver, but for some there's a racial animus." (The Hill, 2014)

Universities across the country also became places where free speech was restricted as college campuses began to create so-called "safe spaces," designated areas where students could shield themselves from uncomfortable or dissenting viewpoints. Usually, safe spaces were the response to outrage among a large group of students who claim to have been "triggered" by an individual or event on campus.

In 2015, numerous universities, including Missouri, Yale, and Michigan, created safe spaces after students claimed they were victims of microaggressions: subtle displays of racial or sexual bias. UCLA law professor Eugene Volokh argued that safe spaces are at odds with the First Amendment. "I think the problem is they're trying to use this word 'safe'—which conveys the image of a violent attack—and turning it into safe from ideas and statements we find offensive," Volokh told *Fox News*. "There is no right to be safe from that."

Legal expert Alan Dershowitz went even further in criticizing the creation of safe zones on college campuses, telling *Fox News* a "fog of fascism is descending quickly over many American universities." (Fox News, 2016) In a *New York Times* article, contributing writer Judith Shulevitz offered some historical context regarding safe spaces: "The theory that vulnerable students should be guaranteed psychological security has roots in a body of legal thought elaborated in the 1980s and 1990s and still read today. Feminist and anti-racist legal scholars argued that the First Amendment should not safeguard language that inflicted emotional injury through racist or sexist stigmatization," Shulevitz wrote. (New York Times, 2015)

Other universities attempted to place literal restrictions on campus speech. In August 2016, Princeton University advised its staffers to no longer use the word "man" as part of an effort to start using "gender-inclusive language." Instead, they were instructed to use words such as "individual," "person," or "people." According to the guidelines complied by Princeton's HR department, "Gender-inclusive language is writing and speaking about people in a manner that does not use gender-based words." (Fox News, 2016)

During the same month, West Virginia University (WVU) informed its 29,000 students that they would be breaking federal law if they refused to use the pronouns preferred by individuals who claimed to be transgender. WVU claimed because the US departments of Justice and Education insist that transgender people are protected by sexual discrimination law, using the wrong pronouns was therefore a crime. The university also provided "a handy guide on proper pronoun usage" that explains how to swap out pronouns such as "he," "him," and "his" for gender-neutral pronouns such as "ve," "ver," and "vis." (Daily Caller, 2016) In an article for breitbart.com, Dr. Susan Berry writes, "The ideological goal of imposing many new pronouns is to blur, stigmatize and outlaw the public's long-standing social and legal distinctions between men and women. Progressives and transgender activists sneer at those distinctions as the 'gender binary.'"

The right to free speech is one of America's most important founding principles. It's the purest means by which to challenge injustices and the most recognizable sign of a truly free society. The nation's media is intended to be a watchdog for the people offering unbiased check of those entrusted with making decisions on their behalf. However, the modern mainstream media has become a permanent arm of the Democratic Party, making its focus the ultimate success of the party rather than the interest of the American people. Nowhere was this more evident than the collusion that took place between the media and the Obama administration. The creations of so-called "safe spaces" on college campuses were attempts by communist entities at the involved universities to accustom students to the idea of living with restrictions on speech. Any attempts to manipulate free speech, whether by attempting to mislead the American people through wordsmithing or by placing literal restrictions on speech, any such manipulation should be vehemently rejected. It's important to remember that the First Amendment was intended to protect controversial speech. Nice speech doesn't need protecting.

Chapter 6

From Marxist Beginnings

In 2007, a little-known Illinois state senator named Barack Obama entered the presidential race. He would win the Democratic party's nomination and ultimately go on to win the general election and become the first African American president of the United States. Obama was arguably the most unvetted presidential candidate in US history, cruising through the electoral process completely unfettered. Thanks to a mainstream media that was clearly in the tank for the Left, there was no one to call public attention to major red flags and inconsistencies in Obama's background. The communist powers-to-be recognized they were dealing with an electorate that was displeased with the current state of affairs and predisposed to embrace a new radical ideology. They simply needed the right package, which came in the form of Obama. The Left used race and the public's discontent with the Republican Party to evoke an emotional response from voters rather than an educated one. Thanks to a compliant mainstream media, voters were fed a constant stream of propaganda that portrayed Obama as an almost Christ-like figure, the one who could save not only America, but the entire world. Vast numbers were drawn to Obama and flocked to the polls to blindly cast votes for a candidate they knew virtually nothing about. Obama was easily elected and wasted no time pursuing his vision for America.

To adequately critique Obama's presidency and its effects on America, one must first understand his political ideology. Virtually all of the main influences throughout Obama's life were socialists/communists who longed to see America transformed into a socialist utopia. Obama's mother, Ann Dunham, was a radical leftist whose background is as full of inconsistencies as Obama's. His father, Barack Obama Sr., was a Kenyan-born Muslim. The two met while both were students at the University of Hawaii. They were reportedly married on February 2, 1961, while Ann was three months pregnant. She filed for divorce on January 27, 1964. She would spend the rest of her life traveling the world, with most of her time spent in Southeast Asia, while leaving Obama Jr. in Hawaii to be raised by her parents. Obama's grandparents were well-to-do and enrolled the young Obama in Honolulu's largest and most prestigious private school. Obama's grandfather was a socialist and would spend time drinking and conversing with other like-minded individuals. One such person was a man named Frank Marshall Davis, a black communist poet and card-carrying member of the Communist Party USA (CPUSA). Throughout his life, Davis wrote for numerous communist publications including the *Chicago Star* and the *Honolulu Record*.

Davis was also the author of the book *Sex Rebel: Black*, a hardcore pornographic novel, he published under the pseudonym Bob Greene. In the book, Davis recounted in explicit detail a series of sexual encounters including bondage, simulated rape, and bisexual encounters. In 1951, Davis was identified as a CPUSA member in a report by the Commission on Subversive Activities to the Legislature of the Territory of Hawaii. The House Un-American Activities Committee (HUAC), an anti-communist congressional committee, also accused Davis of being involved with several communist-front organizations. The FBI kept him under surveillance for nineteen years.

Stanley Dunham took a particular interest in Davis and chose him to be a mentor and father-figure for Obama. Obama's half-sister, Maya Soetoro-Ng, said in an interview with the Associated Press that their grandfather saw Davis as "a point of connection, a bridge if you will, to the larger African-American experience for my brother." In his autobiography *Dreams from My Father*, Obama repeatedly writes about Davis referring to him only as "Frank." He writes about "a poet named Frank" who was full of "hard-earned knowledge" and advice. From the time Obama was ten until eighteen, he was mentored by Davis, influencing his sense of identity. Davis supplied Obama with an abundance of Marxist and anti-American ideas. In the book, Obama recalls meeting with Davis just before leaving for Occidental College in 1979, at which time Davis lectured Obama, saying, "You're not going to college to get educated. You're going to get trained.... They'll train you to forget what you already know. They'll train you so good, you'll start believing what they tell you about equal opportunity and the American way and all that [expletive deleted]." In *Dreams from My Father*, Obama reflects on his senior year as a time of apathy and drug use. "I had learned not to care," he writes. "Pot had helped, and booze; maybe a little blow when you could afford it."

At Occidental College, Obama was a lackluster student at best, and his tendency for drug use had increased as he indulged in alcohol, marijuana, and cocaine. His social circle consisted exclusively of left-wing radicals. In *Dreams from My Father*, Obama writes, "To avoid being mistaken for a sellout, I chose my friends carefully. The more politically active black students. The foreign students. The Chicanos. The Marxist professors and structural feminists."

He was mentored by Lawrence Goldyn, an openly gay political science professor who had a significant influence on Obama's acceptance of homosexuality. At a White House gathering in 2014 to celebrate the "pride" of lesbian, gay, bisexual and transgender (LGBT) people, Obama credited Goldyn for helping shape his thinking on the LGBT rights agenda while at Occidental. "I just wanted to acknowledge him, because he helped shape how I think about so many of these issues, and those sort of quiet heroes that sometimes don't get acknowledged," Obama said of Goldyn. Obama also joined the Students for Economic Democracy (SED), a radical socialist organization. It was at an SED-sponsored rally that Obama gave his first public speech by delivering the opening remarks for the event.

In 1981, Obama transferred to Columbia University, where his proclivity for Marxism increased dramatically. What is known about Obama's time at Columbia is limited to his autobiography and what has been obtained through public records. In his autobiography, Obama mentions that he attended "socialist conferences." "Political discussions, the kind that at Occidental had once seemed so intense and purposeful, came to take on the flavor of the socialist conferences I sometimes attended at Cooper Union or the African cultural fairs," wrote Obama.

After graduating from Columbia University, Obama went on to receive yet another degree from Harvard Law School. After college, Obama worked as a civil rights attorney and taught at the University of Chicago Law School from 1992 to 2004. During his time there, Obama taught the theories and tactics of radical community organizer Saul Alinsky, author of *Rules for Radicals*. Alinsky's tactics were based on the neo-Marxist strategies of Antonio Gramsci. Gramsci's form of transformational Marxism was based on infiltration and gradualism rather than armed revolution. He believed in bringing about changes so subtle that few would notice until it was too late.

In 1985, Obama became a community organizer, working with an Alinsky-affiliated group called Developing Community Projects. Obama was also a paid director of the Woods Fund, which provides funding for the Midwest Academy, an institution that teaches the Alinsky tactics of community organizing. He was elected to the Illinois state senate in 1997 and served until 2004. During his campaign for the state senate, Obama received the endorsement of the Democratic Socialists of America (DSA). Obama was an associate of the Chicago branch of the DSA and a member of the "New Party," a Marxist third party that briefly existed in Chicago from 1992 to 1998. Obama was elected to the US Senate in 2004, where he served until his presidential bid in

2007. Obama's entire senate career, both state and federal, was devoid of any significant legislative achievement.

In his second autobiography, *The Audacity of Hope*, Obama wrote the Constitution "is not a static but rather a living document, and must be read in the context of an ever-changing world." If this doesn't sound familiar, it should. Woodrow Wilson wrote in his treatise "Constitutional Government in the United States," "The trouble with the theory [of limited and divided government] is that government is not a machine, but a living thing. This is where the living and breathing constitution comes from. It is modified by its environment, necessitated by its tasks, shaped to its functions by the sheer pressure of life."

Communist Goal 29. Discredit the American Constitution by Calling It Inadequate, Old-Fashioned, Out of Step with Modern Needs, a Hindrance to Cooperation between Nations on a Worldwide Basis

It is logical to conclude that the communist influences that surrounded Obama from childhood into early adulthood played a dramatic role in the shaping of his world view. The Marxist indoctrination he underwent at the hands of Davis and others influenced the fundamental development of what would become his political ideology. Based on Obama's own admission that while in college, he sought to surround himself with left-wing radicals, it is clear that the indoctrination he received as a child had taken root and was then motivating him as an adult. After college, Obama's affinity for communism only increased as he immersed himself in the radical philosophies of other communist leaders such as Alinsky. This prelude to Obama's political career puts into context the Marxist doctrine he would pursue once elected president of the United States.

Chapter 7

The Fundamental Transformation of America

At a campaign rally in 2008, presidential candidate Barrack Obama shouted to a crowd of supporters, "We are five days away from fundamentally transforming the United States of America." The comment garnered little attention from the mainstream media, but its significance can never be overstated. Even prior to becoming president, Obama had a Marxist vision for America and the determination to pursue his agenda at all costs once elected.

In 2009, the Bureau of Alcohol, Tobacco, Firearms and Explosives (ATF) launched an operation it called Fast and Furious, which consisted of the sale of illegal firearms with the intended purpose of tracking the sellers and purchasers. It is believed the firearms were destined for Mexican drug cartels in an effort by the Obama administration to link the sale of legal firearms in the United States to illegal cross-border activity as part of a new push for gun control. The operation went awry when the ATF lost an estimated fourteen hundred weapons in Mexico, two of which were found at the scene of US Border

Patrol Agent Brian Terry's murder in Arizona. Senate Judiciary Committee and the House Oversight and Government Reform Committee launched a Congressional investigation, during which Attorney General Eric Holder was cited for contempt for failing to turn over documents relating to the Fast and Furious operation. In order to protect Holder from any future prosecution, Obama asserted executive privilege over the requested documents. The House Oversight Committee filed a civil lawsuit against Holder in a further attempt to force disclose of the documents. (CNN, 2016) After more than two years of legal wrangling by the Obama administration, which mired the suit in procedural motions and mediation, Holder announced plans to step down in 2014. (Politico, 2014) In March 2016, Mexican officials raided the hideout of Mexican drug lord Joaquin "El Chapo" Guzman and found a gun that was linked to Fast and Furious. The Department of Justice said in a letter to Congress that a .50-caliber rifle that Mexican officials sent for tracing after Guzman's arrest was connected to Fast and Furious. (CBS News, 2016)

On March 23, 2010, Obama signed into law the Affordable Care Act (ACA), more commonly known as Obamacare. Under the new health care law, Americans would be required to purchase health insurance or pay a penalty for failing to do so. The idea of government forcing the American people to purchase a product, which was the basis for Obamacare, is a direct violation of the Constitution. On June 28, 2012, in the case of *The National Federation of Independent Business v. Sebelius*, the US Supreme Court upheld the constitutionality of the health care law's individual mandate as a tax. All of the most significant promises Obama made regarding the ACA prior to it becoming law proved to be complete lies. Among those included the ACA would not add to the national deficit, individuals who were happy with their health care plans and their doctors could keep them, and small businesses would not see an increase in costs. It's important to note that the increased costs for families and businesses as a result of Obamacare was in addition to a pledge by Obama during his 2008 campaign not raise taxes on anyone making less than $250,000 a year, which also proved to be a lie. In October 2016, the Obama administration admitted that ACA premiums would soar by an average of 25 percent in most states beginning the following year. The ACA, which will always define Obama's legacy as his signature piece of legislation, embodies one of the most basic fundamental ideas of Marxism, which states "from each according to his abilities, to each according to his needs."

Another major failure of Obama's presidency was his foreign policy, which was arguably inept from day one. Perhaps the biggest blunder was Obama's decision in 2010 to pull troops out of Iraq without a status of forces agreement. The decision to pull out prematurely created a power vacuum that many military analysts agree gave rise to the terrorist organization the Islamic State in Iraq and Syria (ISIS). At the time Obama announced the decision to withdraw the troops, he took complete credit for the decision, saying, "So tonight, I am announcing that the American combat mission in Iraq has ended. Operation Iraqi Freedom is over and the Iraqi people now have lead responsibility for the security of their country. This was my pledge to the American people as a candidate for this office."

(NBC News, 2010) He again took credit for the decision in 2011, while announcing the completion of the troop withdrawal. During a White House press briefing, Obama said, "So today, I can report that, as promised, the rest of our troops in Iraq will come home by the end of the year. After nearly nine years, America's war in Iraq will be over." (WhiteHouse.gov, 2011) He even touted the decision as a completed campaign promise during his 2012 re-election campaign. However, despite repeatedly taking credit for the troop withdrawal, in 2014, as Iraq began to deteriorate and ISIS became a serious threat to the region, Obama suddenly denied the decision was his. "What I just find interesting is the degree to which this issue keeps on coming up, as if this was my decision," said Obama. (Town Hall, 2014) He went on to blame former Iraqi Prime Minister Maliki for the decision.

In August 2012, Obama warned that any use of chemical or biological weapons by the Syrian government against the Syrian people would not be tolerated. Obama referred to the potential use of such weapons as a "red line." "We have been very clear to the Assad regime, but also to other players on the ground, that a red line for us is we start seeing a whole bunch of chemical weapons moving around or being utilized. That would change my calculus. That would change my equation," said Obama. The threat of action by Obama implied that if necessary, he would make a unilateral decision to act without the approval of Congress. However, when evidence surfaced in 2013 that Syrian President Bashar Al-Assad had engaged in the use of chemical weapons on his own people, Obama once again shifted his rhetoric. Obama denied having made the "red line" statement, saying, "I didn't set a red line. The world set a red line." (Washington Post, 2013)

He also unexpectedly decided to seek congressional approval for a military strike, which then placed all responsibility on Congress. "This debate is about the world's red line. It's about humanity's red line. And it's a red line that anyone with a conscience ought to draw. This debate is also about Congress's own red line," Obama told reporters. So now it was the world's red line.

In early 2012, the Obama campaign debuted its new slogan for the upcoming presidential election, which was simply "Forward!" The "O" in "Forward!" was featured in the familiar style of the Obama logo. Again, the Obama campaign selected a slogan with communist/socialist roots. It was a commonly used name for many communist/socialist publications throughout the nineteenth and twentieth centuries. In 1905, Vladimir Lenin founded a publication by the name of *Vperyod*, which means "Forward." From 1912 to 1915, Mussolini was the editor *Avanti*, or "Forward," which was the official rag of the Italian Socialist Party. During the same era, the name of the official newspaper of the Social Democratic Party of Germany was *Vorwarts*, which is the German translation of "Forward."

On June 15, 2012, Obama announced that his administration would no longer deport young illegals who matched certain criteria that had previously been proposed under the DREAM Act. As a result, the Obama administration created a new immigration policy called Deferred Action for Childhood Arrivals (DACA). This announcement led to an unprecedented rush of young illegal aliens pouring over the nation's southern border. In November 2014, Obama went further by announcing an executive action to suspend the nation's immigration laws for roughly five million illegal aliens. The executive order applied to undocumented parents of US citizens and residents who had lived in the country for at least five years. In December 2014, US District Judge Arthur Schwab, in Pennsylvania, issued an opinion stating parts of Obama's immigration executive actions were unconstitutional. "President Obama's unilateral legislative action violates the separation of powers provided for in the United States Constitution as well as the Take Care Clause, and therefore, is unconstitutional," wrote Schwab. (Fox News, 2014) In February 2015, Judge Andrew S. Hanen, a federal judge for the Southern District of Texas, ruled in favor of Texas and twenty-five other states that had challenged Obama's immigration actions and immediately halted the programs. (Washington Post, 2015)

Ultimately, Obama's immigration actions were ruled as unconstitutional and stuck down by the courts. The executive branch does not have the power to make laws nor pick and choose which ones to enforce. In March 2016, a report by the Center for Immigration Studies revealed that criminal aliens released by the government between 2010 and 2015 went on to be charged with 124 homicides. "The criminal aliens released by ICE in these years—who had already been convicted of thousands of crimes—are responsible for a significant crime spree in American communities, including 124 new homicides. Inexplicably, ICE is choosing to release some criminal aliens multiple times," wrote Jessica Vaughan, director of policy studies. (Washington Examiner, 2016)

The issue is the real motivation behind Obama's desire to grant amnesty to millions of illegal aliens. He of course claimed it was out of kindness and compassion for people who were simply seeking a better way of life. However, comments by Obama in a January 23, 2015, interview with Vox revealed his true agenda. While discussing how he felt the spread of vibrant social diversity is constricting the GOP's ability to champion conservative causes, such as smaller government and independent families, Obama said he was "hopeful" immigration would drown conservatism. "The Republican Party, even the most conservative, they have much less ability, I think, to express [opposition to single-sex marriage] than they did even ten years ago," Obama said. "The Republican Party, even the most conservative, they have much less ability, I think, to express discriminatory views than they did even ten years ago ... And that's a source of optimism. It makes me hopeful," he said. (Daily Caller, 2015) Clearly, Obama's true reason for wanting to allow millions of illegal aliens to pour into the United States was to bring in millions of new voters for the Democratic Party. If Obama's efforts to change the voting demographics of this country by diluting the conservative vote had come to fruition, it would have made electing a future Republican president virtually impossible.

This same motivation was behind a set of new housing regulations proposed by President Obama during the summer of 2015. According to the Department of Housing and Urban Development (HUD), the initiative was designed to diversify the wealthiest neighborhoods in America while reinvigorating poor communities. Areas that failed to comply with the new rules would risk losing federal funding. According to HUD Secretary Julián Castro, the new rules would give poor families a better opportunity to succeed. (The Hill, 2015) "Unfortunately, too many Americans find their dreams limited by where they come from," said Castro. "This important step will give local leaders the tools they need to provide all Americans with access to safe, affordable housing in communities that are rich with opportunity." In reality, this was simply another attempt by Obama to alter voting demographics in America. Like his effort to bring in millions of illegal aliens to dilute the conservative vote, Obama knew that relocating low-income families, which typically vote Democrat, into wealthier white neighborhoods, which typically vote Republican, would significantly alter the voting demographics of those areas by nullifying what had traditionally been Republican strongholds.

On September 11, 2012, the US Consulate in Benghazi, Libya, was attacked, which resulted in the deaths of US Ambassador Chris Stevens and three others. Top-ranking officials, including President Obama and Secretary of State Hillary Clinton, all claimed it was a spontaneous attack perpetrated by a crowd of demonstrators who were outraged over an obscure Internet video that denigrated the Prophet Muhammad. Following the attack, a number of whistleblowers began to come forward with allegations that contradicted the official talking points of the Obama administration. To this day, questions still abound, fueling suspicions of scandal and cover-up.

Obama's first term consisted of lies, a lack of transparency, and constant attempts to enact Marxist policies. Regarding his economic policies in particular, Obama further burdened an already stagnant economy. According to data released by the US Census Bureau, the real median income of American households decreased by $2,627 and the number of Americans living in poverty increased by approximately 6.7 million during Obama's first term in office. (US Census Bureau, 2013)

In May 2013, the Internal Revenue Service admitted it had targeted conservative and Tea Party groups during the 2012 presidential campaign. They underwent added scrutiny by the IRS after applying to become 501[c][4] organizations and to be granted tax-free status. In October 2013, the American Center for Law and Justice filed a complaint against the United States and the IRS on behalf of forty-one organizations in twenty-two states, which detailed a long-running assault on Tea Party and conservative groups dating back to 2009. The complaint claimed the attacks were orchestrated by senior IRS officials in conjunction with Congressional Democrats and the White House. In May 2013, IRS official Lois Lerner appeared before Congress as part of an open investigation into the matter. Lerner read a statement in which she proclaimed her innocence but then pleaded the Fifth Amendment and refused to answer any questions.

Also in 2013, it was revealed that the National Security Agency (NSA) was engaged in the warrantless collection of Americans' phone calls and emails. The mass data collection was brought to light when former CIA employee-turned-whistleblower Edward Snowden leaked the information to an AP reporter. Under its surveillance program known as PRISM, the NSA forced telecommunications companies to hand over telephone records of millions of US customers. (The Guardian, 2013) Over the following months, Snowden continued to release additional documents, exposing the depth of the NSA's warrantless surveillance practices. In response to growing concerns over the constitutionality of the NSA's surveillance program, the American Civil Liberties Union (ACLU) filed a lawsuit that accused the US government of a process that was "akin to snatching every American's address book." (Washington Post, 2013) In 2014, amid sustained public outrage over the NSA's warrantless surveillance practices, Obama announced the NSA would end its "bulk collection" of telephone records. He added in the future, the NSA would be required to first seek a new type of court order before acquiring data held by telecommunication companies. Despite the change in policy regarding the gathering of Americans' phone records, Obama made no mention of NSA surveillance of the Internet. Clearly, the NSA's surveillance program was unconstitutional and a violation of millions of Americans' privacy rights. However, what was perhaps most telling was Obama's approval of such practices. Obama repeatedly defended the program, claiming it was beneficial to national security.

Another major communist influence that was prevalent throughout Obama's presidency was that of radical community organizer Saul Alinsky. Obama taught Alinsky's theories and tactics at the University of Chicago. In 2008, Alinsky's son praised Obama for applying his father's model of organizing to his presidential campaign. "Obama learned his lesson well. I am proud to see that my father's model for organizing is being applied successfully beyond local community organizing to affect the democratic campaign in 2008. It is a fine tribute to Saul Alinsky as we approach his 100th birthday," said David Alinsky. (Boston Globe, 2008) On March 21, 2013, we see direct evidence of Alinsky's influence on Obama as he channeled Alinsky during an address in Jerusalem; he encouraged young Israelis to bypass their country's leadership in order to "create change you want to see." He told the crowd of college students that Israel "has the wisdom to see the world as it is, but also the courage to see the world as it should be." In his book *Rules for Radicals,* Alinsky used the same phraseology to lay out his main agenda: "It is necessary to begin where the world is if we are going to change it to what we think it should be. That means working in the system." (World Net Daily, 2013)

Obama began 2014, his sixth year in office, by signaling that his tendency to bypass Congress and circumvent the will of the people would soon amplify. On January 14, he once again renewed his pledge to act without Congress if they did not agree with his policy demands. "I've got a pen and I've got a phone," Obama said, "and I can use that pen to sign executive orders and take executive actions and administrative actions that move the ball forward."

On January 22, 2015, Communist Party USA chairman John Bachtell published an essay in which he stated that American communists were eager to work with the Democratic Party as part of a united effort to achieve communist goals. "Labor and other key social forces are not about to leave the Democratic Party anytime soon," Bachtell wrote. "They still see Democrats as the most realistic electoral vehicle to advance their agenda, especially in the national battle against the extreme right."

Communist Goal 15. Capture One or Both of the Political Parties in the United States

In his address at the annual National Prayer Breakfast on February 5, 2015, Obama used the occasion to make an attempt at equating Christianity to radical Islam. "Unless we get on our high horse and think this is unique to some other place, remember that during the Crusades and the Inquisition, people committed terrible deeds in the name of Christ," said Obama. "In our home country, slavery and Jim Crow all too often was justified in the name of Christ." Despite the fact his comments were offensive to Christians, they were rife with inconsistencies. To begin with, his comments regarding the Crusades were misleading, to say the least. The Crusades were defensive wars intended to stop the spread of radical Islam and the senseless killing of innocent Christians living in the Middle East. Sound familiar? As for his comments regarding the Jim Crow era, it's true the Ku Klux Klan attempted to used Christianity as a justification for violence against blacks; however, such atrocities in no way coincided with the teachings of Christianity. This is, of course, in contrast to Islamic terrorism, which is rooted in the teachings of the Koran.

In July 2015, Obama unilaterally brokered a deal with Iran that would lift economic sanctions on the country and place limits on its nuclear program. For its part, Iran agreed to dismantle two-thirds of its nineteen thousand installed centrifuges. However, the deal lacked the means by which to verify whether Iran was upholding its end of the agreement or not. Although Iran agreed to inspections of nuclear sites by the International Atomic Energy Agency, they were to be given twenty-four-hour notice of any inspections. In return for agreeing to limits on its nuclear program, Iran reportedly received between $100 and $150 billion in sanctions relief. Obama later conceded that the release of frozen assets could be used to fund terrorist organizations. "Do we think that with the sanctions coming down, that Iran will have some additional resources for its military and for some of the activities in the region that are a threat to us and a threat to our allies?" Obama said. "I think that is a likelihood, that they've got some additional resources." (Washington Examiner, 2015)

Communist Goal 2. US Willingness to Capitulate in Preference to Engaging in Atomic War

In January 2016, Obama set his sights on befriending another communist country, using his last State of the Union address to call on Congress to lift the trade embargo on Cuba. On March 20, Obama arrived in Cuba, becoming the first sitting president to visit the communist island in eighty-eight years. During a meeting with his Cuban counterpart Raul Castro, Obama told the communist dictator that the embargo on his country would be lifted. During a press conference, Castro criticized US shortcomings to Obama's face and demanded the return of the "illegally occupied" Guantanamo Bay Naval Base. "We find it inconceivable that a government does not defend and ensure the right to health care, education, Social Security with provision and development, equal pay and the rights of children," said Castro. Obama made no effort to defend America against Castro's criticisms. After the meeting, Obama even said he "personally would not disagree" with the communist leader's criticisms of US failings on education and health care. (Washington Times, 2016) Later, Obama posed for photographers in front of an image of notorious Cuban revolutionary Che Guevara.

Communist Goal 4. Permit Free Trade between All Nations Regardless of Communist Affiliation and Regardless of Whether or Not Items Could Be Used for War

The Obama presidency was dominated by his complete dedication to the communist agenda. Obama never strayed from his Marxist ideology nor lost sight of the end result he desired. Due to his determination to enact legislation by executive order rather than working with Congress, Obama failed to put into place any legislation that would last beyond his presidency. Legislation passed by executive order may easily be reversed by the following president, as opposed to that which is passed into law through Congressional approval, which requires congressional action to repeal. Thus, Obama's presidency ended without any major legislative accomplishment to speak of. Obama placed his radical agenda above the oath he took to uphold the US Constitution and act in the best interest of the American people. It was never a matter of what was best for the people but rather what would best further his radical agenda. Obama was willing to use any means to pursue his agenda as long as it led to the desired outcome. This type of consequentialism is often expressed by the phrase, "The ends justify the means." If Obama had simply shifted to the center, in the same way that President Bill Clinton did while in office, he would have been remembered as undeniably one of the nation's greatest presidents.

In 2017 the Pew Research Center released a report titled *How America Changed During Barack Obama's Presidency* which outlined changes that took place during Obama's tenure. According to the report, "A steady hollowing of the middle class, for example, continued during Obama's presidency, and income inequality reached its highest point since 1928." The report also stated that "Those who self-identify as atheists or agnostics, as well as those who say their religion is 'nothing in particular,' now make up nearly a quarter of the U.S. adult population, up from 16 percent in 2007." Regarding the overall moral of Americans, the report stated "financial prosperity – even stability – feels increasingly out of reach to many Americans: Today, far more people are pessimistic than optimistic about life for the next generation of Americans." Despite the lies and corruption throughout Obama's presidency, as evident in this chapter, perhaps the single most honest statement uttered by Obama was his 2008 campaign pledge to "fundamentally transform" America.

Chapter 8

The Failure of the Opposition

Another factor that has allowed the communist Left to gain a foothold within America has been the absence of an opposition party. In the American-style two-party system of government, it is intended that the two parties push back against one another and forge debate until a consensus is reached. The result is hopefully well-rounded legislation that serves the betterment of the American people. Therefore, divisiveness among the two parties is essential to meet the desired result. For too long, the Republican Party has failed to uphold its intended role as a true opposition party, therefore allowing the Left to make great strides toward furthering the communist agenda. At times, the GOP's policies have shown little distinction to that of its leftist counterparts.

While Obama drastically increased the nation's debt, spending more than all previous administrations combined, his predecessor shares a large degree of blame. Although Obama's socialist tendencies were clear, the case can be made that President George W. Bush was a socialist as well, given the expansion of government spending that occurred during the

Bush presidency. Under Bush, the Department of Homeland Security was created, health care was expanded through Medicare Part D, and the national debt increased more than $4 trillion. Although current projections indicate that the national debt will increase to over $20 trillion by the end of Obama's presidency, it is important to acknowledge that out-of-control spending and lack of fiscal oversight began under the Bush administration.

According to data compiled by the Center for Responsive Politics, Morgan Stanley, Goldman Sachs, and Citigroup Inc. were among the top donors to George W. Bush's 2004 presidential campaign. However, all three reappeared as top donors to President Obama's 2008 campaign as well. President Bush was also extensively criticized for his ties to the oil industry, which became the focus of wide-spread accusations regarding his administration and policy making. However, British Petroleum (BP), the fourth-largest oil company in the world (and responsible for the 2010 Gulf of Mexico oil spill), donated more to President Obama's campaign in 2008 than it did to President Bush in 2004. According to the Center for Responsive Politics, BP's campaign donations to the 2008 Obama campaign totaled $71,051 versus that of the 2004 Bush campaign, which totaled $14,370.

Republicans consistently failed to oppose Obama throughout his time in office. There was no better example of this than regarding the national debt. Republicans voted to increase spending every time there was a budget vote and often included any add-ons that Obama wanted. One of the only instances that Republicans took a stand with demands of their own was the 2011 budget showdown, in which they won $2 trillion in spending cuts. However, this proved to be just an anomaly, as Republicans went back to business as usual, caving to Obama's demands each time there was a budget vote. The GOP majority voted to raise the debt ceiling in every subsequent year. The most egregious display of capitulation by Republicans happened in 2015, when they voted to pass an omnibus spending bill, which included funding for the organization Planned Parenthood, the nation's largest provider and promoter of abortion. The GOP-approved spending bill granted funding to Planned Parenthood, freeing the organization of any penalty for its mutilation of unborn babies. From 2011 to 2015, the national debt increased by $3,970,023,503,348 under the Republican-controlled House of Representatives. (CNS News, 2015) Unfortunately, the national budget wasn't the only thing Republicans caved on in 2015. Additionally, they approved a "clean" Homeland Security bill, without any objections to an unconstitutional executive order by Obama that granted amnesty to millions of illegal aliens. Also, the same year, Republicans caved regarding Obama's unilateral nuclear deal with Iran.

The Republican Party has consistently demonstrated a unwillingness to identify the communist influences that exist within the Democratic Party. In 2012, retired Lt. Colonel Allen West, a former Republican Representative from Florida, made headlines when he asserted that up to eighty House Democrats were card-carrying members of the Communist Party. "That's a fair question. I believe there's about 78 to 81 members of the Democratic Party that are members of the Communist Party," said West. (Politico, 2012) Instead of joining West and calling attention to communist operatives serving in the Democratic Party, Republicans gerrymandered West's district in Florida and prevented him from being re-elected.

Republicans consistently criticized Obama for refusing to use the term "radical Islam" when referring to Islamic terrorism. They chided Obama by proclaiming it was impossible to defeat an enemy without first being willing to identify who the enemy is. At the same time, Republicans refused to identify communist members within the Democratic Party.

Americans need the Republican Party to be the opposition party that it was intended to be and fight against any and all attempts by the Left to enact communist policies that seek to undermine America's constitutional form of government. Voters elected Republicans in overwhelming majorities in 2010 and 2014 because they were tired of the communist policies of Barack Obama. Republicans failed to meet the will of voters and did little to curtail Obama's Marxist agenda. Too often, Republicans appeared to be in agreement with their Democratic counterparts, rather than standing in opposition to them. Remember: Whenever the two parties seemingly agree, the American people are probably getting cheated.

Chapter 9

Future Threats to Religious Freedom in America

In 2011, the Pew Research Center's Forum on Religion and Public Life projected the number of Muslims living in the United States to rise from 2.6 million in 2010 to 6.2 million by 2030. (Pew, 2011) The defenders of Islam maintain it is a religion of peace, despite the fact that virtually every act of terror that occurs around the world is carried out by Muslims. The liberal Left in America dismisses this fact by insisting that the vast majority of Muslims are peaceful. Since the terrorist attacks of September 11, 2001, the Left has denounced any concern regarding America's growing Muslim population by asserting that only 1 percent of the country's Muslim citizenry is possibly radicalized. If we accept the estimate that 2.6 million Muslims resided in the United States in 2010, the Left's claim that only 1 percent is radicalized would mean roughly 20,000 Muslims were plotting to kill Americans while living here.

Our other enemies are not so obvious in their intentions to destroy us. Unlike Muslims, they are not driven by a religious ideology, but rather a hatred of religion in general. Instead of Al

Jazeera, they broadcast their twisted propaganda through the liberal mainstream media. Instead of hijacking our airplanes, they've hijacked our courts. They're not as bold as our Muslim counterparts, but they are just as dangerous to our survival. Their goal is to strip the country of all morality.

In 2003, Alabama Supreme Court Chief Justice Roy Moore was forced to remove a display of the Ten Commandments from the rotunda of the Alabama Supreme Court building. In November 2005, teachers at a Georgia elementary school reportedly were told to nix any religious pins and refrain from referring to a party as a "Christmas" party, while the local district censored certain religious Christmas songs from its "winter" program. In December 2005, a Seattle-area school district recalled its December lunch menus because they were printed with the greeting "Merry Christmas." The menus were reprinted with the greeting "Happy Holidays."

Also in December 2005, officials at a New Jersey elementary school changed the words of "Silent Night" in its X-mas Files concert program. Students were encouraged to bring in music selections but cautioned not to choose any "religious" songs. Students were also forbidden from writing "Merry Christmas" in class in English; only the Spanish translation of "*Feliz Navidad*" was permitted. In February 2006, a federal appeals court panel ruled on the side of New York City schools to ban the display of the Christian Nativity during Christmas.

In April 2006, a University of Oregon school newspaper ran a cartoon depicting Jesus on the cross with an erection. In June 2006, a girl who was graduating from Foothill High School in Clark County, Nevada, was denied her diploma after thanking God in her valedictorian speech. Also that same month, the ACLU sued a West Virginia high school over a picture of Jesus that had hung in its halls for over thirty years. In December 2006, the ACLU had a statue of Moses holding the Ten Commandments removed from outside a courthouse in Cumberland County, Tennessee. Berkeley officials were forced to remove a nativity scene from in front of the courthouse, where it had been displayed for over forty years. In Winston-Salem, North Carolina, the ACLU challenged prayer at city council meetings. In December 2007, Southwestern Oklahoma State University mandated "Merry -----mas" as a holiday greeting, banning "Christ." In March 2008, seven Christians were arrested and convicted of disorderly conduct for praying at a gay fest in a public park in Elmira, New York. They were praying silently for the participants of the event, which was celebrating homosexual behavior.

In February 2012, the ACLU filed a lawsuit to have a Ten Commandments display removed from the lawn of a New Mexico courthouse. In April 2012, the Stall Brook Elementary School in Bellingham, Massachusetts, removed the word "God" from Lee Greenwood's "God Bless the U.S.A.," which was to be featured in a school assembly concert. Following outrage by parents, school officials removed the song all together from the fourth grade concert. In August 2013, the New Mexico Supreme Court ruled that two Christian photographers violated the state's Human Rights Act by refusing to photograph a same-sex commitment ceremony. One justice for the case said the Christian photographers were "compelled by law to compromise the very religious beliefs that inspire their lives."

In October 2013, active duty troops attending a briefing at Camp Shelby in Mississippi were told to classify the American Family Association, a well-respected Christian organization, as a domestic hate group due to their advocacy for traditional family values. Two weeks later, soldiers attending a briefing at Fort Hood were told that evangelical Christians and Tea Party members were a threat to the nation and that any soldier who donated to those groups would be punished under the Uniform Code of Military Justice. In May 2014, a Colorado bakery, Masterpiece Cakeshop, was found to be in violation of the state's anti-discrimination laws after the Colorado Civil Rights Commission determined the bakery broke the law by refusing to bake a wedding cake for a same-sex couple. The store was ordered to change its policies immediately and its staff to attend comprehensive training on the state's anti-discrimination laws. The owner of the bakery was also ordered to submit quarterly reports to the commission for the following two years to confirm that his store was not refusing service to customers based on their sexual orientation.

In August 2014, the Orange County Public School District replaced all football team chaplains with life coaches. The school district also banned Bible verses and any references to the Bible on school property. The school district's actions were due to a legal threat filed by the Freedom from Religion Foundation. Also that the same month, the school district in Midlothian, Texas, removed dedication plaques at two of its elementary schools because the plaques contained references to God. The school district made the decision to remove the plaques following a complaint by the Freedom from Religion Foundation.

In September 2014, the Ramay Junior High School in Fayetteville, Arkansas, ordered a thirteen-year-old female student to remove a shirt that read "Virginity Rocks." School officials said the shirt contained sexual content and could cause a "disruption" in the classroom. In October 2014, the examiner for a Lexington Human Rights Commission issued a ruling that the Christian owner of a T-shirt company broke a local law by refusing to print shirts for the Lexington Pride Festival. The hearing examiner stated that the T-shirt company could not discriminate against individuals because of sexual orientation or gender identity, and the owner of the business was ordered to attend diversity training conducted by the Lexington Human Rights Commission. In February 2015, a student at Yulee High School in Nassau County, Florida, was disciplined after he concluded morning announcements by saying, "God bless America." The student was disciplined after the school received a written complaint and threat of legal action from the American Humanist Association. In July 2015, Sweet Cakes by Melissa, a Christian bakery in a Portland, Oregon, suburb, was found guilty of violating the civil rights of a lesbian couple after refusing to bake a wedding cake for the couple. The Oregon Bureau of Labor and Industries claimed to have found "substantial evidence" that the bakery discriminated against the lesbian couple and violated the Oregon Equality Act of 2007. The bakery was forced to close down and ordered by the state to pay $135,000 in damages to the lesbian couple.

Trying to eliminate any reference to God is just one way

liberals execute this attack on Christianity. Another way that has become increasingly visible is their efforts to rewrite history. Efforts are under way to develop "scientific" explanations for things that occurred during biblical times. They believe that if they can scientifically explain biblical miracles, then that eliminates the whole belief that such events were caused by God. For example, in 2000, an Israeli neurologist claimed that Goliath, of the biblical account of David and Goliath, suffered from a hormonal disease. Vladimir Berginer, a professor of neurology at Ben-Gurion University, stated that Goliath was actually suffering from acromegaly, a disease of the pituitary gland, which caused a tumor to swell against his optic nerve. According to the professor's theory, Goliath would have been vision impaired, which would explain how David was able to defeat him.

In April 2006, a Florida State University researcher claimed he had found a "natural explanation" for the biblical account of Jesus walking on the surface of the Sea of Galilee. He theorized that a rare combination of optimal water and atmospheric conditions resulted in a unique, localized freezing phenomenon called "springs ice." "This frozen patch of ice floating on the surface of the lake would have made it difficult to distinguish from surrounding unfrozen water, making it appear as if Jesus were walking on water." He is also known for his theory on the parting of the Red Sea, which he suggested a combination of strong winds and a land ridge could be the explanation. Other examples of this rewriting of history include the change of secular dating abbreviations in textbooks by the Kentucky State Board of Education. "B.C.E., or Before Common Era, and

C.E., for Common Era, have become popular among academics and some historians, largely because B.C., or Before Christ, and A.D., Anno Domini, in the year of our Lord, are based on Christianity." This is, of course, intended to eventually eliminate the traditional Christian-based abbreviations.

Perhaps one of the best examples of the mainstream media's intolerance of Christians was the treatment of former NFL quarterback Tim Tebow. Tebow first entered the NFL after being drafted in the first round by the Denver Broncos. Tebow played backup quarterback for most of his rookie season, before starting the last three games of the year. The following year, Tebow began the 2011 season again as a backup but became the team's full-time starting quarterback by the sixth game of the season. The Broncos, which had a 1-4 record, began winning after Tebow became the starter, often overcoming deficits late in the game. Tebow led the Broncos to their first AFC West title and first playoff win since 2005. Despite Tebow's accomplishments on the field, he became the subject of constant criticisms for what his critics claimed was his lack of ability.

However, the attacks on Tebow seemed to have less to do with his ability and more to do with his public profession of Christianity. In August 2011, CBSSports.com national columnist Gregg Doyel criticized Tebow in an article. Although Doyel attempted to make the case for why he believed Tebow would never be successful as an NFL quarterback, his comments focused instead on Tebow's faith. "He'll make it in this league—for the Bible tells him so," Doyel wrote. "From the outside it looks like Tebow equates his love for God in heaven with tangible rewards here on earth. And that's more than wrong. It's blasphemy."

Tebow indirectly responded to the criticism by posting "Joshua 1:19" on his Facebook page, which reads, "Have I not commanded you? Be strong and courageous. Do not be afraid; do not be discouraged, for the LORD your God will be with you wherever you go." In November of that same year, former Broncos quarterback Jake Plummer was interviewed on talk-radio show in Phoenix; he criticized Tebow for talking about his faith during postgame interviews. "I wish he'd just shut up after a game and go hug his teammates," said Plummer. "I think that when he accepts the fact that we know that he loves Jesus Christ then I think I'll like him a little better. I don't hate him because of that, I just would rather not have to hear that every time he takes a good snap or makes a good handoff."

Despite finishing the season 8–8, plus a playoff win, the Broncos made the decision to trade Tebow to the New York Jets. Although Broncos president John Elway cited the team's pursuit of veteran quarterback Peyton Manning as the reason for the trade, clearly the incessant criticism of Tebow played a significant role.

Tebow responded by saying, "First and foremost, I just want to thank the Denver Broncos for my time there.… I understand what they were going through. You don't get many opportunities to have a chance to sign Peyton Manning. What a great quarterback he is."

The attacks on Tebow only increased after his arrival in New York. Throughout the season, players, coaches, and commentators described Tebow as a "distraction." Jets cornerback Darrelle Revis claimed Tebow's arrival would only further worsen the team's problems with disorganization. "It was a circus [last season], and it's going to be more of a circus with him in the locker room," Revis said.

"He handles his detractors with Gandhi-like poise," said former NFL defensive end Howie Long. "When Tim Tebow comes, he comes with great distraction," Long told WFAN's Boomer Esiason and Craig Carton.

Seattle Seahawks head coach Pete Carroll told KIRO-AM in Seattle that having Tebow on their team was "just a distraction."

Other media pundits admitted Tebow was hated for his outspoken Christianity rather than his questionable mechanics. Former Cincinnati Bengals wide receiver and TV commentator Cris Collinsworth argued that Tebow has been hated because of his faith and lamented that Tebow was "a guy we're going to vilify."

Stephen A. Smith, who has been critical of Tebow as a quarterback, argued in a similar vein: "When they look at the common athlete, and they say that there is no way they can live up to that; you know, you're wearing your religion on your sleeve, you're getting down on one knee, you're praising God at every turn—which I applaud, by the way—you're doing all these things, you're celibate, you're not going to engage in—oh, people aren't trying to hear that! They don't want to be subjected to those kinds of standards because in their heart of hearts, they don't want to be forced to have to live up to it."

Daniel Foster of National Review Online blamed the hatred against Tebow on his clean lifestyle, which flies in the face of fans' jaded conception of athletes. "People aren't upset at

Tebow's God talk. They're upset that he might actually believe it," wrote Foster.

And in an online column for *USA Today*, Larry Taunton said of the QB's detractors, "Their dislike for Tim Tebow is not, as they would have us believe, about his throwing motion or his completion percentage; it's all about his open professions of faith and his goody-two-shoes image." (Media Research Center, 2011)

After acquiring Tebow, the Jets had an unproductive season; they rarely used him on the field and cut him as soon as the season ended. However, despite his departure from the team, he continued to receive attacks. Former NFL quarterback Jeff Garcia told *USA Today*, "Having Tebow there [last season] just became more of a distraction, more of a circus show.... From an outsider looking in, having Tebow there doesn't bring anything positive. It just brings distraction."

Jets offensive guard Willie Colon told reporters, "I think having the Tim Tebow circus out of here, and having different things that were kind of holding this team back, are starting to go out the window. I think we're all starting to care about football and only football, which is a good sight to see."

It was clear Tebow's NFL career was over, as noted by Yahoo Sports reporter Michael Silver, who quoted two anonymous NFL coaches who stated they would not sign Tebow because of the "circus" that accompanied him. "'He seems like a great guy to have on a team, and I'd be tempted to bring him in as our backup,' one NFC head coach told me Wednesday," wrote Silver. "'But it's just not worth dealing with all the stuff that comes with it.' Or, in the words of one AFC head coach to whom I spoke recently: 'You don't want to put up with the circus.'"

During his first year in the league, Tebow had the top-selling jersey in the NFL and the fastest-selling rookie jersey in NFL history. The following year, after news that Tebow had been named the team's starter, ticket sales spiked, even for away games. When the Broncos traveled to Miami to play the Dolphins for what would be Tebow's first game as a starter, the Dolphins saw a boost in ticket sales, which had been sagging due to the team's winless record. By week 15 of the season, which featured a much-anticipated home game versus the New England Patriots, Broncos ticket sales had increased by 44 percent, according to a 2011 article by Ticketnews.com. The article stated, "In general, the Tebow Effect has helped Broncos ticket prices rise 44 percent since he was named the starter on October 12. The average price for Broncos tickets sold through SeatGeek before that date was $108; now it is $156." In other words, the circus that followed Tebow generated significant revenue, not only for the Denver Broncos organization, but for the NFL as a whole. This means the NFL and all of its subsidiaries were willing to throw away a significant revenue stream simply because they could not tolerate Tim Tebow's expression of his Christian faith.

The bottom line here is, Tim Tebow was driven out of the NFL largely due to his Christian faith. Any accurate assessments of his mechanics at the quarterback position were simply a means by which to criticize him without revealing the real source of the criticisms. Describing the media obsession that followed Tebow as a "circus" was a politically correct way of referring to and bashing his largely Christian fan base.

During ESPN's broadcast of the 2014 NFL draft, the sports network included live coverage of Michael Sam, the first openly gay player to enter the league. After news broke that Sam had been selected by the St. Louis Rams, the live airing featured Sam kissing his partner and shoving cake in one another's face as they celebrated. As if the televised kiss wasn't enough, ESPN later featured a report on Sam's shower habits. At the 2015 ESPY Awards, ESPN presented Bruce Jenner with the Arthur Ashe Award for Courage in recognition of Jenner's decision to come out as transgender. The network defended the decision in an official statement by saying it was "proud" to honor Jenner for "embracing [his] identity and doing so in a public way to help move forward a constructive dialogue about progress and acceptance." Obviously, the mainstream media has no problem embracing homosexuals and transgendered people, but Christians such as Tim Tebow are not shown the same tolerance.

Another source of criticism, which is becoming more commonplace, stems from individuals who claim to be Christians themselves. This has become particularly common among celebrities who identify as Christians but use their celebrity status as a platform to criticize other Christians, who take a more biblically accurate stance on social issues. In June 2012, country singer Carrie Underwood stated her support for gay marriage in an interview with the *Independent*, a British newspaper. "As a married person myself, I don't know what it's like to be told I can't marry somebody I love and want to marry," she told the newspaper. "I can't imagine how that must feel. I definitely think we should all have the right to love, and love publicly, the people that we want to love." Underwood emphasized that her stance on the issue was influenced significantly by her church's support for gay marriage. Stating that her church was one of a growing number to adopt the divisive stance, Underwood said, "Our church is gay friendly." She went on to give her personal view of Christianity, which she described in very liberal terms. "Above all, God wanted us to love others," she told the British publication. "It's not about setting rules, or [saying] 'Everyone has to be like me.' No. We're all different. That's what makes us special. We have to love each other and get on with each other. It's not up to me to judge anybody."

In a February 2013 issue of *Allure* magazine, Underwood once again spoke out in favor of homosexual marriage. "I'm in favor of acceptance, "she told the magazine. "And I am a Christian person, and I do love the Lord, and I feel no matter who you are, what you believe, how you live your life, it's not my place to judge."

In an October 2014 interview with *Billboard* magazine, legendary country singer Dolly Parton not only spoke out in support of the homosexual community, she also criticized what she described as "judgmental" Christians. "They know that I completely love and accept them, as I do all people," Parton said, regarding her gay following. "I think everybody should be allowed to be who they are, and to love who they love. I don't think we should be judgmental." Parton went on to criticize Christians who may visit her family theme park Dollywood, which is known as a favorable destination spot of the LGBT community. "It's a place for entertainment, a place for all families, period," she said. "But as far as the Christians, if people want to pass judgment, they're already sinning. The sin of judging is just as bad as any other sin they might say somebody else is committing."

Notice both Underwood and Parton frequently use the word "judgmental" to criticize Christians who refuse to accept homosexuality, as instructed by the Bible. Judgement regarding homosexuality as well as other sexual sins has already been determined by God. Christians who refuse to accept homosexuality are simply following God's instruction. Those who call themselves Christians and claim to support homosexuality, such as Underwood and Parton, are in clear violation of God's word. Yet there is a growing trend among Christian leaders and churches to do just that.

In September 2013, Pope Francis criticized the Catholic Church for being "obsessed" with abortion, gay marriage, and birth control. "The church's pastoral ministry cannot be obsessed with the transmission of a disjointed multitude of doctrines to be imposed insistently," said Francis.

In October 2013, Russell Moore, head of the Southern Baptist Convention's Ethics and Religious Liberty Commission, made headlines after he suggested that Christians should concede surrender in the culture wars. In an interview with the *Wall Street Journal*, Moore said Christians should "tone down the rhetoric and pull back from the political fray." In June 2014, the Presbyterian Church (USA) voted to change its definition of marriage and allow its pastors to perform gay weddings in states where same-sex marriage is legal.

What is to blame for this trend in Christians to accept worldly ideas and behaviors that violate biblical instruction? Have Christians simply become complacent as a result of decades of passivity regarding major societal issues? Or has the communist movement achieved its stated goal of infiltrating the church and bringing about its downfall from within?

In 2016, WikiLeaks published thousands of emails belonging to John Podesta, campaign chairman for then Democratic presidential nominee Hillary Clinton. In one particular email, Podesta and Sandy Newman, president and founder of the Progressive nonprofit Voices for Progress, casually discussed fomenting "revolution" in the Catholic Church. "There needs to be a Catholic Spring, in which Catholics themselves demand the end of a middle ages dictatorship and the beginning of a little democracy and respect for gender equality in the Catholic Church," wrote Newman.

In his response, Podesta assured Newman that organizations already existed specifically to infiltrate the Catholic Church with Progressive ideology, but cautioned that the time was not right for full revolution—just yet. "We created Catholics in Alliance for the Common Good to organize for a moment like this. But I think it lacks the leadership to do so now. Likewise Catholics United. Like most Spring movements, I think this one will have to be bottom up," wrote Podesta. (Lifezette, 2016)

Communist Goal 27. Infiltrate the Churches and Replace Revealed Religion with "Social" Religion. Discredit the Bible and Emphasize the Need for Intellectual Maturity, which Does Not Need a "Religious Crutch"

Christians today are extremely misguided regarding self-defense, due to misinterpretations of scripture or a complete lack of understanding altogether. The Bible is full of passages that justify not only the use of physical force but even killing when done in self-defense. It has become commonplace for Christians to argue against any act of self-defense while citing scripture as justification for their position. However, such passivity is proven erroneous by an accurate interpretation of scripture. The passage most commonly used by Christians to argue against self-defense is Matthew 5:39, which involved turning the other cheek. This is, of course, a complete misinterpretation of scripture. The passage refers to a personal insult and not a physical attack. At the time, striking someone on the right cheek, usually in the form of a backhanded slap, was a Jewish form of insult. In no way does the passage instruct Christians to subject themselves to violent aggression. Another go-to verse used by Christians to justify pacifism is the Sixth Commandment. The commonly used English version, which reads "Thou shalt not kill," seems clear at face value. However, the original Hebrew translation of the passage read "Thou shalt not commit murder." To understand the true context of the passage, one must understand the difference between moral killing and immoral killing. Moral killing is done in self-defense against an attacker. Immoral killing refers to taking the life of an innocent human being, which is murder. We not only have a biblical right to defend ourselves, the Bible actually mandates it. Various passages instruct Christians to defend themselves and others against violent aggressors. For example, Leviticus instructs us not to stand idly by while our neighbor's life is at stake; Exodus gives you permission to kill an intruder found breaking into your house at night. Perhaps the passage that stands out the most contains an edict from Christ himself. In Luke 22:36, when Jesus was giving his last words of instruction to his disciples before the crucifixion, he said to them, "And he who has no sword, let him sell his garment and buy one."

According to a 2014 Gallup survey, over three-quarters of Americans identify as Christian. Yet, as the majority, we allow our religious liberties to be continuously violated. Society has no regard for Christianity, and its hostility towards Christians grows increasingly vigorous. I believe the world does not respect us, partly because it does not fear us. Respect is often times accompanied by fear. As children, we are taught right from wrong, and it is out of fear of the consequences that we do not disobey. We are not respected because there is no fear of repercussions otherwise. In April 2006, the Comedy Central television network barred its popular *South Park* series from showing an image of the Islamic prophet Muhammad. However, in the same episode, it allowed a scene in which an image of Christ defecated on the American flag. The network issued a statement, saying, "In light of recent world events, we feel we made the right decision." Even small-minded, degenerate individuals such as those at the Comedy Central network had enough fear for the religion of Islam to avoid disrespecting it in the slightest way.

Christians in America must become more combative in response to personal attacks and the growing infringement of our constitutional right to religious freedom. Whether it is referred to as "respect" or "fear," Christians must acquire it. If allowed to go unabated, the current encroachment on religious liberties will ultimately erode the constitutional rights of Christians to worship and express their religious views openly and freely.

Conclusion

America currently finds itself in a state of moral decline, purposely brought about by the communist movement, with some contribution by other ideological groups seeking to eradicate Christianity. While the average American has spent the past several decades preoccupied with sports and pop culture, the communist movement has quietly pursued its agenda, creating cultural changes so gradual that virtually no one noticed. With the election of Barrack Obama, and signs that decades of incremental Marxism were finally beginning to bear fruit, the communist Left became more emboldened and intensified its efforts of the complete takeover of America. While some Americans have begun to take notice, many still remain oblivious to the growing force that threatens the future of the United States as we know it.

Each generation of Americans is tasked with preserving the United States as a free nation. Unfortunately, recent generations, beginning with the baby boomer generation, have failed to combat the gradual dismantling of America's constitutional framework. If Americans continue to demonstrate such passivity and apathy, there will come a point at which Americans will be forced to choose between radical revolt or falling under the heavy hand of communism. It is crucial that Americans wake up now, while there is still time to reverse our present course through legal and legislative means.

The bedrock of American society has long been the traditional nuclear family. However, traditional families have been devastated by decades of attacks from the communist Left. The nuclear family has been a major target of communism, dating back to Karl Marx, who referred to it as the "bourgeois family" and called for its abolishment. One of the best examples of such attacks on the traditional nuclear family in America has come by means of the radical homosexual movement. The legalization of same-sex marriage by the US Supreme Court on June 26, 2015, was a direct assault on the sanctity of traditional marriage. Put aside the fact that the Supreme Court only has the power to interpret laws, not create them, which makes the ruling unconstitutional, the real question is, what was the need for such a law in the first place? In many states, same-sex couples were already granted the same rights as married couples under the title of civil unions. States that did not yet recognize civil unions would eventually have been forced to do so, based on a prevailing legal trend in favor of granting rights to same-sex couples. Therefore, the only discrepancy between traditional married couples and same-sex couples was the difference in title (i.e., "civil union" versus "marriage"). Why the concern over the title, if the real issue was equal rights? The answer is, the real goal of the radical homosexual movement was never equal rights but rather to attack traditional marriage. And what better way to have a devastating effect on the nuclear family than to erode the sanctity of traditional marriage? Other factors that have had a negative effect on traditional families include the welfare state, the radical feminist movement, and the promotion of promiscuity through movies and TV shows. If America is to ever return itself to any semblance of a moral society, we must vehemently defend the traditional nuclear family and restore it as the bedrock America desperately needs it to be.

The education of America's youth must always be a top priority if we are to secure the country's future. The hearts and minds of any nation's young people are always a major target of any communist movement that seeks to take over said nation. Article I, section 8 of the US Constitution, which grants the federal government all of its powers, does not give the federal government any power to control education. Therefore, the US Department of Education should be abolished, and all control of public education should be transferred to state and local governments.

A greater increase in parental involvement is also needed to repair our nation's flawed educational system. For too long, parents in the United States have abdicated their parental responsibility by ceding control of their children's education to the federal government. Parents must re-engage themselves in the education of their children in order to monitor curriculum and guard against any possible indoctrination. Particular emphasis should be given to history education to ensure that students are taught a fact-specific curriculum. Proper knowledge of US history is essential in order to promote a healthy sense of nationalism among America's youth.

Parents also have the responsibility to teach their children within the home and provide them with morals, which cannot be acquired through public education. A recent study published in the journal *Sage Open* stated that the percentage of Americans who claim they never pray reached an all-time high in 2014, up fivefold since the 1980s. Over the same time period, belief in God and interest in spirituality appears to have similarly declined, especially among young adults. The findings suggest that "millennials are the least religious generation in memory, and possibly in American history," said Jean M. Twenge, psychology professor at San Diego State University and lead researcher for the study. (Vocativ, 2016) In order to preserve America's future, it is imperative that we provide younger generations with the knowledge and morals needed to become productive members of society. The importance of this was understood by President Ronald Reagan, who said, "Freedom is never more than one generation away from extinction."

There is no doubt America is politically divided, arguably more so now than ever before. The popular opinion is that the division is due to a radical shift to both the right and left of the political spectrum. I would argue instead the only radical shift that has taken place has been to the Far Left. Conservative ideas, which are referred to as that of the extreme right wing, are not radical; they are the ideas that America was founded on. If our founding fathers were alive today, they would be labeled "right-wing extremists." However, the reality is the only radical shift to occur has been to the Far Left, which is due to the takeover of the Democratic Party by the communist movement. The ideas regarding the future of America held by today's Democratic Party are in contrast to that of the founding fathers and therefore anti-American.

When left to our own devices, human beings are ugly creatures, capable of barbaric acts. It is only through some sense of morality that we restrain the inherent sin that exists within each of us from birth. Every civilized society requires a system of laws to control and protect against criminal acts. However, without morality, even laws break down, failing to preserve civility and leading to the ultimate breakdown of society. As sinful beings, we require morality to restrict the selfish and wicked desires that otherwise lead to barbaric behavior. This is a concept that was understood by many of our founding fathers, particularly John Adams, who said, "Our Constitution was made only for a moral and religious people. It is wholly inadequate to the government of any other."

One indicator of a moral society is how its people treat one another. We've allowed ourselves to be divided by superficial issues, which can only breed envy and hatred for one another. While this has been orchestrated by the communist movement to cause division among the masses, we must not allow ourselves to turn against one another. Our enemies understand that we are at our weakest and easiest to conquer when we are divided. One thing fascism does not do is discriminate. It seeks to suppress everyone equally. We must stop allowing ourselves to be divided in terms of race, economic status, and sexual orientation and start seeing one another as fellow Americans. If we allow ourselves to be divided, we will ultimately perish together. As Abraham Lincoln stated, "A house divided against itself cannot stand."

It is important to note that being moral does not require you to also be religious. Although the two are often incorrectly equated with one another, morality is not synonymous with religion. Anyone can be moral, even the most devout atheist. But since morality is a key component of religion, Christians should take on the lead role of returning America to a more moralistic society. However, leading America in a moral rejuvenation will require Christians to first regain the ability to stand up for themselves against growing attacks from the communist Left. Communists have long viewed religion as standing in the way of their ability to gain complete control of a nation. For communism to exist, the people must look to government as the supreme entity from which all rights are given. Any belief in something bigger than government is detrimental to the existence of communism. For this reason, communists must not allow the existence of any belief system other than that of the communist ideology. In recent years, attacks on Christianity in America have increased. Christians can expect to see such attacks continue to increase as the communist Left grows more emboldened. It is imperative that Christians, specifically Christian men, stand up in defense of the constitutional rights of all religious Americans. A failure to do so will render the moral rejuvenation within America virtually impossible. The effort to reinstate America's moral prudence will ultimately require winning the battle against the growing threat to religious freedom.

The belief in a creator was also paramount as one of the fundamental ideas established in the founding, as necessary for the existence of a free society, as stated in the Constitution.

The idea that all rights are derived from a creator rather than mankind is fundamental to the American form of constitutionally limited government. The absence of a belief in a creator allows for the rights of mankind to be dictated by other men. This was emphasized by Thomas Jefferson, who stated, "God who gave us life gave us liberty. Can the liberties of a nation be secure when we have removed a conviction that these liberties are the gift of God?"

Today's America has become a place where facts no longer matter, public opinion is heavily swayed by media-driven narratives, and morality is denounced in the name of ultra-tolerance. The Constitution is criticized as being an outdated document that should either be altered to accommodate changing times or discarded all together. This present culture of relativism threatens to dismantle the values and principles that America was founded upon and have sustained it ever since. The rights contained in the Constitution are specifically stated as having been granted by God rather than mankind. They are absolute and therefore not subject to conditional terms or interpretations. Should mankind be the one to give us our rights, then mankind has the power to take them away. If America hopes to remain a free nation, perhaps it should heed the words of President Ronald Reagan: "If we ever forget that we are one nation under God, then we will be a nation gone under."

1. "100 years of collective dementia," World Net Daily, last modified January 4, 2013, http://www.wnd. com/2013/01/1913-2013-100-years-of-collective-dementia/

2. "The Great Society 50 Years Later," The Daily Signal, last modified May 22, 2014, http://dailysignal.com/2014/05/22/ great-society-50-years-later-failing-americas-poor/

3. "Communist agenda makes its way to our mainstream," Idaho Press-Tribune, last modified January 14, 2008, http://www. idahopress.com/bestread/communist-agenda-makes-its- way-to-our-mainstream/article_6740861e-0b59-5a0e-8e4d- 0724bea87f7f.html

4. "The Saudi Guide To Piety," Washington Post, last modified July 22, 2008, http://www.washingtonpost.com/wp-dyn/ content/article/2008/07/21/AR2008072102357.html

5. "U.S. Commission Wants Saudi-Funded School Closed Until Textbooks Can Be Reviewed," Fox News, last modified October 19, 2007, http://www.foxnews.com/story/2007/10/19/ us-commission-wants-saudi-funded-school-closed-until- textbooks-can-be-reviewed.html

6. "U.S. Religious Knowledge Survey," Pew Research Center, last modified September 28, 2010, http://www.pewforum. org/2010/09/28/u-s-religious-knowledge-survey/

7. "The State Against Blacks," The Wall Street Journal, last modified January 22, 2011, http://www.wsj.com/articles/SB100 01424052748704881304576094221050061598

8. "17% black teens live with parents, 54% for whites," Washington Examiner, last updated February 12, 2015, http://www.washingtonexaminer.com/report-just-17-black-teens-live-with-parents-54-for-whites-both-low-marks/article/2560151

9. "The dark, intolerant, and abusive nature of the gay agenda," Renew America, last updated April 28, 2004, http://www. renewamerica.com/columns/hutchison/040428

10. "America Had More Married Couples With Kids in 1963 Than in 2014," Town Hall, last updated July 1, 2015, http://townhall. com/columnists/terryjeffrey/2015/07/01/america-had-more-married-couples-with-kids-in-1963-than-in-2014-n2019742/page/full

11. "Teen Promiscuity Linked to TV," Catholic Exchange, last updated September 14, 2004, http://catholicexchange.com/teen-promiscuity-linked-to-tv

12. "Universities Look To Mainstream Polyamory," Daily Caller, last updated May 2, 2016, http://dailycaller.com/2016/05/02/across-country-universities-look-to-mainstream-polyamory/

13. "Do you know why Earth Day is April 22?" World Net Daily, last updated April 19, 2012, http://www.wnd.com/2012/04/do-you-know-why-earth-day-is-april-22/?cat_orig=us

14. "Terrorist Professor Bill Ayers and Obama's Federal School Curriculum," Accuracy in Media, last updated September 21, 2012, http://www.aim.org/special-report/terrorist-professor-bill-ayers-and-obamas-federal-school-curriculum/

15. "Study: Common Core ELA Standards Will Further Harm U.S. History Instruction," Pioneer Institute, last updated September 2, 2014, http://pioneerinstitute.org/featured/study-common-core-ela-standards-will-further-harm-u-s-history-instruction/

16. "The College Board's Attack on American History," Breitbart, last updated May 28, 2014, http://www.breitbart.com/big-government/2014/05/28/the-college-boards-attack-on-american-history/

17. "Primetime propaganda: Liberal writers 'hijacked top shows such as Friends, The Golden Girls and even SESAME STREET to push left-wing agenda,'" Daily Mail, last updated June 2, 2011, http://www.dailymail.co.uk/news/article-1393499/Primetime-propaganda-Liberal-writers-hijacked-shows-Friends-The-Golden-Girls-SESAME-STREET-push-left-wing-agenda-book-claims.html

18. "Obamacare Propaganda in TV Scripts?" Town Hall, last updated April 4, 2014, http://townhall.com/columnists/brentbozell/2014/04/04/obamacare-propaganda-in-tv-scripts-n1818639/page/full

19. "Juan Williams Suggests 'All-White' Tea Partiers Driven By Racism," Daily Caller, last updated August 3, 2014, http://dailycaller.com/2014/08/03/juan-williams-suggests-all-white-tea-partiers-driven-by-racism-video/

20. "Eric Holder Plays Race Card," Free Beacon, last updated April 9, 2014, http://freebeacon.com/politics/eric-holder-plays-race-card/

21. "Holder sees 'racial animus' in opposition," The Hill, last updated July 13, 2014, http://thehill.com/blogs/blog-briefing-room/news/212082-holder-sees-racial-animus-in-opposition

22. "'Safe spaces' on college campuses run at odds with First Amendment, say law experts," Fox News, last updated November 14, 2014, http://www.foxnews.com/us/2015/11/13/safe-spaces-on-college-campuses-unconstitional-say-law-experts.html

23. "In College and Hiding From Scary Ideas," New York Times, last updated March 21, 2015, http://www.nytimes.com/2015/03/22/opinion/sunday/judith-shulevitz-hiding-from-scary-ideas.html?_r=3

24. "University implements man ban," Fox News, last updated August 19, 2016, http://www.foxnews.com/opinion/2016/08/19/university-implements-man-ban.html

25. "West Virginia University: Calling Someone The 'Wrong' Prounoun Is A Title IX Violation," Daily Caller, last updated August 21, 2016, http://dailycaller.com/2016/08/21/west-virginia-university-calling-someone-the-wrong-prounoun-is-a-title-ix-violation/

26. "Income, Poverty, and Health Insurance Coverage in the United States: 2012," US Census Bureau, last updated September 2013, http://www.census.gov/prod/2013pubs/p60-245.pdf

27. "Operation Fast and Furious Fast Facts," CNN, last updated September 26, 2016, http://www.cnn.com/2013/08/27/world/americas/operation-fast-and-furious-fast-facts/index.html

28. "House seeks contempt for Holder," Politico, last updated October 2, 2014, http://www.politico.com/story/2014/10/eric-holder-new-contempt-fast-and-furious-111572

29. "Fast and Furious gun found at El Chapo hideout," CBS News, last updated March 16, 2016, http://www.cbsnews.com/news/fast-and-furious-gun-found-el-chapo-hideout-mexico/

30. "NSA collecting phone records of millions of Verizon customers daily," The Guardian, last updated June 6, 2013, http://www.theguardian.com/world/2013/jun/06/nsa-phone-records-verizon-court-order

31. "ACLU sues over NSA surveillance program," Washington Post, last updated June 11, 2013, https://www.washingtonpost.com/politics/aclu-sues-over-nsa-surveillance-program/2013/06/11/fef71e2e-d2ab-11e2-a73e-826d299ff459_story.html?utm_term=.fbf4ec195012

32. "Son sees father's handiwork in convention," Boston Globe, last updated August 31, 2008, http://archive.boston.com/bostonglobe/editorial_opinion/letters/articles/2008/08/31/son_sees_fathers_handiwork_in_convention/

33. "Obama quotes Alinsky in speech to young Israelis," World Net Daily, last updated March 21, 2013, http://www.wnd.com/2013/03/obama-quotes-alinsky-in-speech-to-young-israelis/

34. "Federal judge: Obama immigration actions 'unconstitutional,'" Fox News, last updated December 17, 2014, http://www.foxnews.com/politics/2014/12/17/federal-judge-obama-immigration-actions-unconstitutional.html

35. "Federal judge in Texas blocks Obama immigration orders," Washington Post, last updated February 17, 2015, https://www.washingtonpost.com/news/morning-mix/wp/2015/02/17/federal-judge-in-texas-blocks-obama-immigration-orders/

36. "Obama "Hopeful" Immigration Will Drown Conservatism," Daily Caller, last updated February 9, 2015, http://dailycaller.com/2015/02/09/obama-hints-immigration-will-drown-conservatism/

37. "Obama's full speech: 'Operation Iraqi Freedom is over,'" NBC News, last updated August 31, 2010, http://www.nbcnews.com/id/38944049/ns/politics-white_house#.Vs6xbq9OKK0

38. "Remarks by the President on Ending the War in Iraq," WhiteHouse.gov, last updated October 21, 2011, https://www.whitehouse.gov/the-press-office/2011/10/21/remarks-president-ending-war-iraq

39. "President Who Pulled U.S. Troops Out of Iraq Says Idea He Pulled Troops Out of Iraq is 'Bogus,'" Town Hall, last updated August 11, 2014, http://townhall.com/tipsheet/katiepavlich/2014/08/11/president-who-pulled-us-troops-out-of-iraq-says-he-didnt-pull-troops-out-of-iraq-n1877290

40. "President Obama and the 'red line' on Syria's chemical weapons," Washington Post, last updated September 6, 2013, https://www.washingtonpost.com/news/fact-checker/wp/2013/09/06/president-obama-and-the-red-line-on-syrias-chemical-weapons/

41. "Obama admits Iran deal could fund terror,"
    Washington Examiner, last updated July 15,
    2015, http://www.washingtonexaminer.com/
    obama-admits-iran-deal-could-fund-terror/article/2568354

42. "124 illegal immigrants released from jail later
    charged in 138 murder cases," Washington
    Examiner, last updated March 14, 2016, http://www.
    washingtonexaminer.com/ice-124-illegal-immigrants-
    released-from-jail-later-charged-in-138-murder-cases/
    article/2585720

43. "Obama lets Castro criticize U.S. shortcomings,"
    Washington Times, last updated March 21, 2016, http://www.
    washingtontimes.com/news/2016/mar/21/castro-demands-us-
    give-back-guantanamo-lift-embarg/?page=1

44. "New Obama housing rules target segregated neighborhoods,"
    The Hill, last updated July 8, 2015, http://thehill.com/
    regulation/administration/247180-new-housing-rules-target-
    segregated-neighborhoods

45. "Boehner-Obama Spending Deals Have Increased Debt
    $3,970,023,503,348.07," CNS News, last updated October
    26, 2015, http://cnsnews.com/news/article/terence-p-
    jeffrey/boehner-obama-spending-deals-have-increased-
    debt-397002350334807

46. "West: 80 communists in the House," Politico, last updated
    April 12, 2012, http://www.politico.com/story/2012/04/
    west-80-commies-in-the-house-075025

47. "The Future of the Global Muslim Population," Pew Research
    Center, last updated January 27, 2011, http://www.pewforum.
    org/2011/01/27/the-future-of-the-global-muslim-population/

48. "USA Today Ignores Anti-Religious Hatred of Tebow," Media Research Center, last updated December 6, 2011, http://newsbusters.org/blogs/paul-wilson/2011/12/06/usa-today-ignores-anti-religious-hatred-tebow

49. "WikiLeaks: Podesta and Left-Wing Activist Plot 'Catholic Spring,'" Lifezette, last updated October 12, 2016, http://www.lifezette.com/polizette/wikileaks-podesta-left-wing-activist-plot-catholic-spring/

50. "Americans Skeptical Of God But Think Heaven Is Real, Somehow," Vocativ, last updated March 21, 2016, http://www.vocativ.com/news/299168/americans-pray-think-heaven-is-real/

87036872R00071

Made in the USA
Middletown, DE
01 September 2018